797,885 Books

are available to read at

Forgotten Books

www.ForgottenBooks.com

Forgotten Books' App
Available for mobile, tablet & eReader

ISBN 978-1-332-11893-9
PIBN 10287192

This book is a reproduction of an important historical work. Forgotten Books uses state-of-the-art technology to digitally reconstruct the work, preserving the original format whilst repairing imperfections present in the aged copy. In rare cases, an imperfection in the original, such as a blemish or missing page, may be replicated in our edition. We do, however, repair the vast majority of imperfections successfully; any imperfections that remain are intentionally left to preserve the state of such historical works.

Forgotten Books is a registered trademark of FB &c Ltd.
Copyright © 2015 FB &c Ltd.
FB &c Ltd, Dalton House, 60 Windsor Avenue, London, SW19 2RR.
Company number 08720141. Registered in England and Wales.

For support please visit www.forgottenbooks.com

1 MONTH OF FREE READING

at
www.ForgottenBooks.com

By purchasing this book you are eligible for one month membership to ForgottenBooks.com, giving you unlimited access to our entire collection of over 700,000 titles via our web site and mobile apps.

To claim your free month visit: www.forgottenbooks.com/free287192

* Offer is valid for 45 days from date of purchase. Terms and conditions apply.

English
Français
Deutsche
Italiano
Español
Português

www.forgottenbooks.com

Mythology Photography **Fiction**
Fishing Christianity **Art** Cooking
Essays Buddhism Freemasonry
Medicine **Biology** Music **Ancient Egypt** Evolution Carpentry Physics
Dance Geology **Mathematics** Fitness
Shakespeare **Folklore** Yoga Marketing
Confidence Immortality Biographies
Poetry **Psychology** Witchcraft
Electronics Chemistry History **Law**
Accounting **Philosophy** Anthropology
Alchemy Drama Quantum Mechanics
Atheism Sexual Health **Ancient History**
Entrepreneurship Languages Sport
Paleontology Needlework Islam
Metaphysics Investment Archaeology
Parenting Statistics Criminology
Motivational

DEER-STALKING

BY

AUGUSTUS GRIMBLE

Illustrated

LONDON: CHAPMAN AND HALL
LIMITED
1886

[*All rights reserved*]

PRINTED IN ENGLAND.

RICHARD CLAY & SON
BREAD STREET HILL, LONDON,
Bungay, Suffolk.

PREFACE.

WITH the single exception of Mr. Scrope's *Deerstalking in the Scottish Highlands*, the writer is not aware of any book devoted entirely to the subject; certainly of none written with a view of initiating the beginner into the minutiæ of this most fascinating of sports. I have met those who ridicule it, and have protested they would derive as much pleasure in shooting a donkey on Hampstead Heath as in pursuing the wild red deer across the Border. On further inquiry it usually turns out that these scoffers have never even seen a wild deer, and are rashly condemning a sport they have no knowledge of. Others there are who, possessed with no love of sport of any kind, talk in a similar strain; but these are those who hunt not, shoot not, and neither do they fish, and mock at all sports alike. Of other writers on the subject, Mr. Colquhoun in his charming book, *The Moor and the Loch;* Mr. St. John in his *Wild Sports of the Highlands*, both devote chapters to deerstalking, and give much useful and valuable information. Mr. McDonald, in his *Cattle, Sheep, and Deer*, also renders a short account of the pleasures to be enjoyed and the hardships to be endured by the deerstalker, but he does not enter into the subject with a view of being of any assistance to the tyro. I have also lately read with pleasure and profit *A Handbook of Deerstalking*, by Alexander Macrae, late forester to Lord Henry Bentinck, with Introduction by Horatio Ross, Esq.

As I read this trio of formidable names, my heart fell within me for fear the ground I was treading should be cut from under my feet. On perusal of Macrae's book my anxiety was relieved, for though all that he says is good and to the point, he does not enter closely into detail. For the sake of those interested in the subject, I must freely confess it is unfortunate for them, but lucky for me, that Mr. Horatio Ross's contemplated book as mentioned in his introduction has been allowed to remain unwritten; had he carried out his intention, the pleasure I have derived from putting these pages together would have been denied me; for all I have to say would have been anticipated.

The late Mr. Bromley Davenport, in his excellently well written *Sport*, devotes two chapters to stalking: one to the chase of the totally wild animal, and the other to the pursuit of the Scotch red deer. He compares the former with the latter to the disadvantage of the Scotch sport, and I do not dispute but that he is correct. When, however, one reads his chapter on the Home Sport, none can doubt but that all his energies were in the chase, and that no thought of tameness crossed his mind at the moment. At any rate Scotch deerstalking is so exciting that no excuses need be made for those who cannot from a variety of reasons go further afield.

Mr. Scrope's book most truly contains a very great deal of valuable information, conveyed also in a style which carries the reader right away on to the mountain tops, and into the burns and peat-bogs he so graphically describes. But Mr. Scrope's book was written a hundred years ago, in the days of single barrel and muzzle-loading rifles. Carefully did the present writer study it before he ever levelled his rifle at a stag, and after a short experience of the sport, the idea impressed itself on him that Mr. Scrope had taken for granted his reader would be already acquainted with many small matters connected with it; daily little facts cropped up which were not mentioned in Mr. Scrope's work, but all of which if known would contribute to success; therefore, without in any way attempting to compete with him, or any of the other mentioned writers, either in style or stalking experience, the writer has thought he could yet be of service to the numbers of young stalkers every year brings to the front.

Each successive season produces a quota of fresh blood—some, the privileged and lucky ones, to join in the sport on actually "cleared" or forested ground; others, the more numerous body, to partake of it on sheep walks marching with some forest; which ground the deer often prefer for better and sweeter grass, or for greater shelter. On such shootings the deer are usually seen and reported by the shepherd, who generally constitutes himself, with great pride, stalker for the occasion, and right well he usually acquits himself. In a first stalk a small idea of what was taking place, an inkling even of how best to take the shot, could not but add doubly to the pleasures of that never-to-be-forgotten day, one's first stag. Failing to understand anything about it, all the pleasure of the actual outwitting his quarry is lost to the novice; he is astonished and hardly knows where to look when the rifle is placed in his hands, and with a whispered "tak' plenty o' time," he is waved forward to go in and kill.

There is nothing new in these pages, and any one who has stalked for a few years knows all that is to be said, and the smallest idea of instructing those who are already old hands is earnestly disclaimed.

These pages are dedicated, in memory of many hard days and many pleasant evenings, to all those friends who have ever given the writer a shot at a stag; but especially to Henry Spencer Lucy of Charlecote Park, Warwick, and Sir Robert Bateson Harvey, Bart., of Langley Park, Slough. To the kindness of these two good friends the writer principally owes it, that for many seasons past he has had the pleasure of pursuing the wild red deer over some of the most difficult and beautiful parts of bonnie Scotland.

A. G.

Windsor,
  July, 1886.

CONTENTS.

	PAGE
PREFACE ...	v

CHAPTER I.
The Rifle and the Spy-glass ...

CHAPTER II.
Clothing—Ponies—Condition—Lunch ... 19

CHAPTER III.
Peculiarities of Deer ... 25

CHAPTER IV.
The Stalk—The Shot ... 31

CHAPTER V.
Wounded Deer — Deer-hounds and Collies— Weights of Deer—"Flesh, Fish, and Fowl" —The Gralloch 48

CHAPTER VI.
A Double Event—My First Stag, and a Memoir of Leger Day, 1875 ... 67

CONTENTS.

CHAPTER VII.

A Fine Weather Stalk, with Wind and Light and Luck all in our Favour, and how September 3rd, 1881, I killed my first "Royal," getting him Home that same Evening — 79

CHAPTER VIII.

A Day with Everything against us: Bad Weather, Bad Luck, and Bad Shooting ... 90

CHAPTER IX.

Stalking en luxe—A long Day in a large Forest with varying Luck — 97

CHAPTER X.

A few Hints to Foresters—Anecdotes of their Gentlemen—Conclusion ... 107

LIST OF ILLUSTRATIONS.

EIN SECHSUNDSECHSIG ENDER	*Frontispiece*
THE BEST SPYING POSITION	*to face p.* 33
A DOWNHILL SHOT ...	37
AN UPHILL SHOT ...	41
A FOURTEEN POINTER	56
MY FIRST ROYAL ...	87

DEER-STALKING.

CHAPTER I.

THE RIFLE AND THE SPY-GLASS.

In the present day the double-barrelled ·450 breech-loading express rifle is the weapon most usually carried by the deer-stalker. In price they range from twenty to seventy pounds. If you are a Mr. Longpurse, at about the latter figure, Henry, Rigby, Grant, or Purday will give you all you can desire in the way of build, finish, and sighting, and you never need "fash yoursel" about the shooting—it is certain to be straight.

There are also plenty of other most excellent rifle makers, and one has but to study the advertising columns of the *Field* to meet with all one requires. If you belong to the far more numerous but equally honourable family of the Shortpurses, to which the writer himself is all too closely allied, then you must use your judgment where you purchase, and even though it cost some days and considerable trouble, do not buy without shooting the rifle yourself at the target, use a rest, and have the cartridges loaded in your presence, and see that the loads are correct.

This is mentioned because some gun-makers have been known to take gentlemen to see their *guns* shot at the plate with the most wonderful results for pattern and penetration—results which the gun quite fails to maintain when it is sent home. This is how it is managed. Having arrived at the shooting-ground, the would-be purchaser is asked whether he would like to see the gun first tried for pattern or penetration. Suppose the former is chosen, the gun is forthwith loaded, and both barrels are emptied at the three-foot circle with grand results. Then comes the trial for penetration; the brown paper pad is suspended on the plate, both barrels are again discharged, and once more the result is extraordinary. Forthwith in exchange for a cheque the gun becomes Mr. Buyer's own.

Now the truth is, that when tried for pattern the cartridge contains, say two drams of powder and one and a quarter ounces of shot; when tried for penetration the cartridge holds, say four drams of powder and only three-quarters of an ounce of shot!

The writer feels somewhat chary about telling this story, but he is very credibly informed that this trick has been played on inexperienced buyers by unscrupulous gun-makers, and it is mentioned to put the unwary on their guard. With a rifle such a ruse would not have anything like the same effect; but even in trying a rifle it will always be best to see that each cartridge contains what it professes to do.

The ·500 bore and the ·450 bore each have their partisans, but the latter is the rifle most usually carried. It is hardly necessary to say that the ·500 bore, whether with solid or expanding bullet, is by far the most powerful weapon of the two. The average weight of the ·450 bore is about eight pounds and three-quarters, that of the ·500 bore about nine pounds and a quarter; both rifles can, however, be made fully half a pound lighter, although this causes a proportionate increase in the recoil.

In the Highlands you seldom carry the rifle for any considerable distance, so that half a pound more or less need not be much consideration. We have the well known racing dictum that weight will bring a race horse and a jackass together, the former being in this case represented by your stalker; there is, therefore, no reason for using a very light weapon, and the full weight makes a fairer handicap. If your coat, lunch, flask, and spare cartridges be added to this, it will be none too much, for in ninety-nine cases out of a hundred the forester will be in far better walking order than his "gentleman."

A Highlander accustomed to the work will comfortably carry a weight that seems appalling if taken on to one's own shoulder; and yet he will easily walk ahead of his gentleman. I well remember a west coast keeper, who having worked his dogs and carried the bag all day as it was filled, would "jaunt" home beside me for five miles or more, with twenty brace of grouse over his shoulder and the spare cartridges to boot!

The writer is strongly of opinion that where a ·500 bore is used the expanding bullet should be discarded *entirely*; even if planted in the right spot it destroys and renders unfit for the table a good deal of the neck and shoulders, and if by chance striking a little far back, the haunches rarely escape being cut about. The writer has a vivid reminiscence of seeing the extraordinary force of a Purday ·500 bore solid bullet. A *coup de grâce* was fired at a wounded royal at quite close quarters, and the bullet passed right through the horn, which was of great thickness, about six inches above the coronet, and drilled a hole as clean as if a centre-bit had been used. In spite of the great shock this must have given, the stag jumped up and dashed away as if unhurt; the bullet from the second barrel laid him low, and not till we went up to him did we see the effect of the first shot.

With the same rifle the writer also knew the stag shot at to be killed dead, the bullet passing right through the heart and body; another stag in the line of fire was shot through the neck, and a third one beyond received a broken hind leg, and all three were put into the larder.

The writer has placed his trust in the ·450 rifle of Mr. Rigby; they shoot a bullet about seventy grains heavier than those made by other makers; in fact the Rigby bullet is fully a quarter of an inch longer than any other ·450 bullet. The extra weight ensures a greater shock to the animal struck by it, and in cases of having to shoot a long shot across a high wind, less allowance has to be made for windage. With regard to the use of the hollow or expanding bullet in the ·450 rifle, they are decidedly more deadly than the solid one; fewer wounded deer are likely to escape, as the breaking up of the bullet cuts the arteries in all directions, and profuse bleeding ensues at once. Should, however, the shooter have the bad luck to hit a deer in the fore or hind leg, it is far better *for the deer* if he be wounded with a solid bullet.

Unless a clever dog be of the party, the stag will frequently make good his escape, and quickly recover from the wound of a solid bullet; but if struck by an expanding one, the bone will be so smashed, and the tendons so much cut, that it will wither and fall off, and then when winter comes, and the snow cannot be scratched away to uncover his food, he will surely die. Furthermore, against the use of the hollow bullet, with even the ·450 bore, there are many who urge with good reason that, unless the deer be struck just in the right place, and sometimes even then, they render the meat very bloody and quite unfit for table.

The writer has found it a good plan to take out both sorts of bullets, and to load the rifle as the end of the stalk is neared, being guided in the choice by the position of the quarry. If, for instance, it is a solitary stag, or two or three together, and they are *quite* unsuspicious, and the ground shows that unless they move there is every prospect of getting to a hundred yards before firing, the first barrel should carry a solid bullet, everything pointing to an easy quiet shot where no difficulty should be found in planting the bullet within an inch or so of the right spot. If, however, the stalk is for one particular stag with thirty or forty others with him, and perhaps double that number of hinds, a hollow bullet should be placed in both barrels, as the chances are the shot will have to be taken at from one hundred and fifty to two hundred yards, and will be a difficult, quick, and hurried one. With the large charges of powder used in the express rifle of the present day the same sighting will be equally good whether the solid or hollow bullet be used.

As illustrating the difference of the wound and injuries inflicted by the two bullets, the writer one day, being overtaken by dense mist as soon as he had arrived on his beat, and all chance of using the spyglass being at an end, sat down in a deer pass to "wait till the clouds rolled by." Having sat for nearly three hours in the driest and most sheltered spot to be found, sandwich and flask were produced, but hardly ready, when the mist lifted, and the horns of a good stag were seen coming through the pass about one hundred and twenty yards distant. He was trotting fast, having clearly been disturbed, and although straight down-hill, offered a very pretty broadside chance. Snatching the rifle, already loaded with a solid bullet, from the cover, there was barely time to pull back the stops and take a hurried shot. The stag rolled over and lay kicking, and as we were on the point of running in, another one appeared in the tracks of his leader, and instant attention was directed to him. On seeing his struggling companion he turned sharply back, and a short but unsuccessful dash was made to cut him off, which he easily defeated. Returning hastily to the first stag, we found he had recovered his legs, was already out of shot, and in a few minutes was across the march. Pulling out the glasses we could see he was struck far back through the kidneys, and we watched him go for quite two miles.

THE RIFLE AND THE SPY-GLASS.

In travelling this distance he twice fell down and laid for some time, and eventually we saw him hide in a hole, where in all probability he died. As the forest adjoining was rented by gentlemen we did not know, we felt bound, with great regret, for fear of spoiling their sport, to leave him to his fate. The day following this mishap, a long shot at about one hundred and eighty yards presenting itself at a stag running across the shooter, the bullet oddly enough struck exactly the same place as in the stag just mentioned as escaping from a wound with a solid one; but in this latter case when the stag fell he was quite powerless to rise again, the hollow bullet having severed the arteries in all directions, and causing half-a-dozen internal wounds for the one of the solid bullet; and these two shots well exemplify the difference of the power and shock of the two projectiles; and as the bullet in each case was placed some eighteen inches behind the heart, they also most clearly showed the writer he was not shooting far enough in front of running deer.

To put a wounded stag out of his misery a solid bullet should be used; with regard to this style of *coup de grâce*, the writer holds it far more merciful and much quicker to put a bullet through a wounded animal's neck, than to go through the struggling operation of one of the party holding the horns and the other cutting the throat. It is much the best plan to use the rifle, unless, and which is very seldom the case, there are other deer at hand which have not heard the first shot and might be disturbed by a second one.

The length of the ·450 express rifle barrel varies

from twenty-six to thirty inches—it is a matter of taste. The short ones are more convenient, pleasanter to shoot with, and come quicker on the mark; they are also slightly less weighty and more comfortably carried, and less liable to the danger of catching the muzzle against rocks or boulders in a run, and easier to keep out of harm in a long tramp home in the dark, when stumbles if not downright falls are unavoidable.

There are also some gentlemen who use the ·360 bore rifle, but the bullet is so small that unless planted exactly in the heart it is not deadly; if so placed, of course it is as deadly as a larger one. It was with a ·360 bore, fitted with the telescopic sight, that Mr. Edward Kennard made his run of kills, as related in *The Field*, this last autumn. It is, however, the opinion of many that the use of the telescopic sight makes the shooting of deer too easy. *If the quarry will only keep still* it is apparently brought almost within touch of the muzzle of the rifle, and missing becomes nearly impossible. All the difficulties of judging distance, all the nicety of taking the sight in bad light, all the pleasure in fact of making a brilliant shot with the ordinary rifle is done away with, and whether this is to be desired is certainly a debatable point, and resolves itself into a matter of taste. These rifles seem more suited to sport in distant climes which are visited by the traveller but once in a lifetime, where shots are few and far between, and where missing a rare beast may be an opportunity lost for ever; but they seem a mistake for deer in Scotland, which if missed one day will live to show more sport on another one. It should be mentioned that the telescopic sight cannot be used on large bore rifles, as the recoil of the telescope on the eye strikes it far harder than is pleasant or even safe.

And now as to the all-important matter of the rifle sights. It is often stated that the man who shoots brilliantly at game rarely is a good rifle shot, but all the experience of the writer is dead against this theory. Doubtless one can with practice learn to shoot well at a mark with any sight; for the sighting of a rifle only requires learning by plenty of shots and close and careful observation. Practise, practise, practise! if you want to become a dead shot,—at a mark on the level, at sea-birds on a smooth sea, at rocks and stones, up-hill and down-hill and across valleys,—and by degrees a perfect knowledge will be gained as to what sort of a sight should be taken, that is, how much of the foresight should be seen to ensure a hit at the distance a mark is judged to be. It is quite possible to take out a gun to the heather or the stubble, and without ever having had it in the hand before, or fired a shot out of it, good practice if not quite brilliant shooting may be made; but with a rifle used against deer for the first time this would be almost impossible.

The most common sight is the V sight, and the more obtuse the angle of the V the easier it is to use it.

The whole matter, however, when actually shooting at deer is so totally different from firing at a mark, that the sight which serves best for the target is hardly any guide to that most suited for actual service. In shooting at deer the firing position is generally cramped, the time for aiming very short, and except the stalk has been made on a side wind, it is blowing straight into the eyes, and if any rain is falling, that is also following the wind and meeting the shooter's face. Given a dull grey light, a mark to shoot at almost indistinguishable from the background, plenty of ups and downs across which to judge the distance, and it is far easier to make a miss than a kill. To a marksman who is able, with the sun at his back, on a nice fine day to place every shot in the bullseye of a clear white target with a jet-black centre this may seem almost past belief.

All sights for sporting purposes should be made "thick": the cut A will show what is meant by a *thick* sight set exactly right for a shot at a hundred yards—

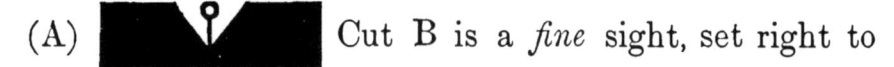

(A) Cut B is a *fine* sight, set right to ensure a hit at a similar distance—(B)

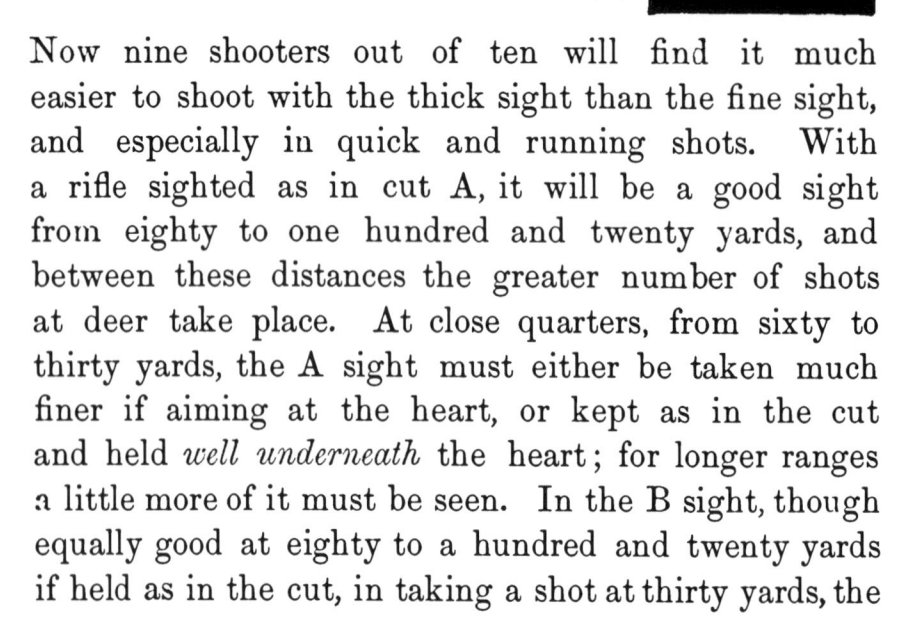

Now nine shooters out of ten will find it much easier to shoot with the thick sight than the fine sight, and especially in quick and running shots. With a rifle sighted as in cut A, it will be a good sight from eighty to one hundred and twenty yards, and between these distances the greater number of shots at deer take place. At close quarters, from sixty to thirty yards, the A sight must either be taken much finer if aiming at the heart, or kept as in the cut and held *well underneath* the heart; for longer ranges a little more of it must be seen. In the B sight, though equally good at eighty to a hundred and twenty yards if held as in the cut, in taking a shot at thirty yards, the foresight would have almost to be *lost to view* if aiming direct at the heart, and this is a very difficult matter to remember and put in practice quickly. Also with the fine sight, and the difficulties of light, &c. already mentioned, it is hard to *keep it fine*. The deer is often so dim that the shooter wants to see a little more of it—the head is raised ever such a trifle, the sight becomes a thick one, the trigger is pressed, and the bullet either ploughs up the peat or smacks on the stones, quite true in direction, but just over the back of the quarry. As a matter of fact, the history of most misses with both barrels may be summed up in three words *over and under*. Personally speaking the writer has found a bar sight the best, with the V inverted and filled in either with enamel, platina, or ivory; as to which is preferable, much depends on the peculiarities of vision of the shooter, and many first-class shots at deer can never shoot well with this description of sight. Of the three substances, that which gives the least "glint" in sunshine will be the best. Ivory discolours with weather, age, and grease, but as long as it is *quite* fresh it beats all others. If some enamel could be made of the eggshell type, dull, pale cream-coloured, and not liable to be affected by wear, it would be better than any of the three mentioned. Mr. Rigby is quite aware of this, and first mentioned the matter to the writer, but at present such a composition has not been produced. He was also the first to point out the great difference there is in visibility between platina and enamel, which any one can see for himself by placing an egg and a highly-polished silver table-spoon on the turf in the dusk.

When walked away from the egg will remain much longer visible than the spoon. The writer has found a platina back-sight with enamel foresight best suited to his own particular vision.

The cut here shows the bar sight set to a hundred yards— A shade more of the foresight being seen makes it good up to two hundred yards. For quick aiming and liberty of vision there is no sight to compare with this.

There is also another sight in use by some stalkers which speaks for itself— The nick above the ivory or platina A is exactly filled by the foresight at a hundred yards. It is not, however, so handy for quick shots as the bar sight or the obtuse V sight.

There are many other fancy sights, but none of them so well adapted for quick shooting, and the three described are those most commonly used for stalking. They and the other varieties can all be seen by going the rounds of the different rifle-makers.

Let no one carry a rifle for stalking as pursued in the Highlands that has no stops to it; anything more dangerous than crawling without them would be difficult to imagine, and they are absolutely necessary for perfect safety. Of course they may, and perhaps should be, dispensed with for tiger-shooting off an elephant, or for other big game shooting, where no stalking has to be done, and when you may become the assailed instead of the assailant, but for Scotch stalking they are indispensable. Some rifles have the stops made to push forward, others to draw back, but those that are made to push forward, and put the stop on behind the hammer, are perhaps the most handy. When the stops are about to be used, care should be taken to hear the "click" of the half-cock, so that it is *certain* the scear has laid hold of the half bent. In badly made rifles, or in those which have seen a great deal of service, or have had the "pull" altered by inexperienced workmen, if this precaution be neglected, it is possible to push the stop into the notch of the hammer before or after it is really at half-cock, and then when it is withdrawn an accidental discharge must take place, and nothing can be more dangerous or disconcerting. The quite modern weapons are made with rebounding locks, which add materially to comfort and safety: it would require the exertion of a double action to cause an accidental discharge with these locks, for the trigger would have to be pressed backwards, and the hammer knocked or pressed forwards, before the cartridge could be exploded; there is, however, no knowing what may happen in a hasty crawl in rough ground, so that it is as well to be on the absolutely safe side, and have stops to the rifle even if made with rebounding locks.

Let the rifle cover be made of stiff material; the brown canvas of which the cartridge bags are made is very good, if tipped with leather to receive the muzzle. The stoutness of the canvas protects the rifle from blows and scratches, and wet only has the effect of making this cover stiffer even than it is when dry. With a case of this description, left unstrapped at the end, the rifle can be extracted very quickly in case of a sudden chance of a shot, and as in some grounds such present themselves several times in the course of each season, this is an advantage not to be despised.

The thin shepherd's plaid mackintosh covers often used are so flimsy, whether wet or dry, that they cling to the rifle, and it is a matter of some seconds before it can be drawn out, and the fact of being in a hurry to do this does not tend to help matters.

Some foresters object to the hard thick cover as making a "crunching" noise when dragged after them in a crawl through heather, and certainly on the rare occasions of *quite* still days it does make a small amount of noise when so carried.

It is quite safe to carry the rifle loaded in the cover with the stops on.

Never forget that a rifle is totally different from a gun, and requires more care to keep it in a state of perfection. A good stalker will clean his gentleman's rifle before he changes his clothes or has his supper. Especially after a wetting great care should be given to the perfect cleansing of the grooving, the muzzle, and the triggers, and when hung up in a room where peat fires are burnt, an old handkerchief should be laid over the triggers to keep the peat dust from getting into them.

In putting a rifle away for the season never plug up the muzzles with rag or tow, whether greased or not it is a most fertile source of rust. In laying a rifle by the great thing is elbow-grease. After well oiling the insides of the barrels rub them out with dry tow till they are quite warm, and the insides shine like silver, and then if put in a dry place it will not want touching for months. When oiling the locks or triggers take care to remove the old oil before applying fresh : if this be not done the old oil will form into small hard lumps, and cause the delicate parts to wear unevenly.

The best way is perhaps to send it to the maker, or follow the plan of an eccentric gentleman who, though in possession of a large income, at the end of each shooting season sends his whole battery to "his uncle's," borrowing a merely nominal amount on their value ; his reason for so doing being that the law of the land compels that relation to take all and every care of anything entrusted to him ! An impecunious scion of a good family heard of this, and was so much struck with the utility of the proceeding, that at the end of a shooting season he did likewise. But, alas, when the next twelfth of August came round—Epsom, Ascot, and Goodwood all having been disastrous—he found himself minus the wherewithal to redeem his guns and rifles, and in the absence of "the governor" abroad, the family butler was taken into confidence, and a bundle of the family spoons deposited in lieu of his battery enabled him to proceed to the North : once there, two months of economy soon put matters right, and no one was ever the wiser ; but he does not now think quite so highly of this plan, and since then has trusted religiously to his gun-maker to keep all in good order.

Having chosen a rifle, the next thing is to procure a good "spy-glass" or telescope. The best are made by Ross of Bond Street, they have a larger field, sharper definition, and more power than any others the writer has met with. The lenses are so arranged that they can be kept to the eye for ten minutes or a quarter of an hour without in any way dimming the sight or making the eye giddy, and at the end of a long spy with one of these glasses it is as ready and quick to take the foresight of the rifle as if none had been used. When made of aluminium they are apparently expensive, as their price is twenty guineas. This metal is, however, a very difficult one to work in, and up to the present no means of soldering it have been discovered, so consequently all the tubes of each tele scope have to be cut from the solid piece, and there is a fortune awaiting any one who can discover a solder for this extraordinary light and beautiful metal. The same description of lenses mounted in brass can be had for rather less than half the cost of the aluminium one, and many prefer these, maintaining that the extra weight keeps them steady, and renders them easier to use in a high wind, and that also they are not so liable to get out of order. If you stick to your own glass, carry it yourself, and keep it *solely* for your own use, an aluminium one will last a life-time. Stalkers and gillies are apt to be a little rough, for they are accustomed to brass-mounted glasses, which will stand a lot of hard usage, and can with impunity be torn open in a moment and shut up with a snap bang.

The writer has never found any difficulty in keeping an aluminium glass in order, or in holding it steady in a wind, and the *great* difference in weight between the two metals is well worth consideration in a hard day's work.

THE RIFLE AND THE SPY-GLASS.

Binoculars of any sort are not of much use, as they cannot be made powerful enough to distinguish stags and hinds at any great distance. The power of a glass is determined by the length of "draw," and telescopes can of course be made much longer than any binocular. It is as well to carry a small piece of wash-leather in the waistcoat pocket to polish the glass with if it should be dim or dusty, and this should be kept free from grit, so that the lenses may not be scratched.

Should it be necessary, as is often the case, to spy in a shower of rain, dry the glass as well and quickly as possible with a handkerchief before shutting it up, and on returning home unscrew the eye-piece and the object-glass, wipe them quite dry and put them in a drawer, then pull out the telescope to its extreme length, and leave it all night in some warm place, but do not expose it to any great heat. A glass well taken care of will rarely refuse to open and shut comfortably; if a strong pull has to be used to open it, or a hard push given to shut it, such force is most apt to injure the fine screws of an aluminium one, the metal being somewhat brittle. It may be mentioned that this metal will not stand a very hot climate like India.

There are plenty of good glasses to be had a great deal cheaper than those mentioned. In a forest a light brass glass with a smaller field is as good as anything, for there you can usually "pick up" the deer with the naked eye at great distances. Even if the eye miss them, so large are the herds, and so well known the places that certain winds will move the deer to, that it becomes almost impossible to miss them with any sort of glass. It is on sheep ground that the glass with the large field is of the greatest service—ground which may have been spied for four or five days in succession without seeing a sign of a deer, but which on the sixth may hold three or four stags, or perhaps a solitary one, which might easily be passed over with a glass having a small field by shifting it too quickly and missing the very spot where the deer are.

When putting a telescope away at the end of the season be careful to choose a perfectly dry place. If a glass be laid by in damp for any length of time, the oxygen of the air actually corrodes the lenses, and gives them an opalesque coating which can only be removed by repolishing; and although such a mishap does not render the glass totally unfit for use, it spoils the sharpness of the definition and dims it to a great extent.

CHAPTER II.

CLOTHING—PONIES—CONDITION—LUNCH, ETC.

RIFLE and glass now being ready, a few words on the above subjects may not be amiss. Walk fairly lightly clad, and have garments rather neutral in colour than very bright or very dark. Greyish homespuns or tweeds having a little yellow or blue in them are usually very invisible; the cap should fit close to the head, and be of the same material. Choose some stuff that will not turn black when wet through; most of the Lovat mixtures, which when dry are of such a good colour for the hill, will turn quite black when soaked with rain. Discard linen shirts of any sort, and wear the best flannel. Have thick woollen stockings, exactly fitting the feet, and whether boots or shoes be worn over them, do not let the soles be too thick, and let the leather round the ankles be very soft and pliable. Whether wearing boots or shoes, on no account use those that are waterproof, for in the course of the day it will be certain that a sea is shipped, and then if waterproofed the moisture stays in all day, not to mention the "sqoosh, sqoosh" each foot makes for many paces afterwards. It is almost needless to say, have plenty of nails in the boots or shoes. Prevention being better than cure, if any one fears blisters at the commencement of the season they may usually be avoided by scraping a little soap off a tablet and applying it *outside* the stocking to the ball of the great toe or the heel, or wherever the tenderness be dreaded.

Knickerbockers are the pleasantest to walk in, but not made too large or baggy at the knee, or they hold such a lot of water after a wet crawl that it runs down and fills the boots, and they also take longer to dry than those cut less voluminously. Do not wear knicker-breeches, which are the fashion at present, for in going up-hill they pull on the knee, and, however slightly, it will tell at the end of a long day or in a long run.

The pockets of the coat should all be made to button—this little precaution will save the loss of many a cigar-case, pipe, or flask. During a rapid slither downhill and the coat-tails flying round your ears, all that is in the pockets may be lost. An old cover coat or a light-coloured mackintosh made in the same shape is the best wrap to take out. If any heavier sort of coat is carried, and only the stalker is with you, it makes a severe burden for him. Of course if your attendants consist of a pony and man, a gillie and a stalker, short of a hot bath you can carry pretty well what you please. These are luxuries that do not fall to every one, though they are often the accompaniments of most big forests. And now if my reader be a poor Sassenach, let me exhort him not to put on a kilt to stalk in; the dress can hardly be a comfortable one for pony-back, and knees that are bared but for a few weeks each year are apt to look blue and cold; granite rocks are hard and sharp to crawl over without long practice, and even burnt heather is not altogether a bed of roses; also skinned and bleeding knees are not a pretty sight to enter the breakfast-room if ladies be of the party, and altogether picturesque as the dress may be, it is best left to those who are to the manner born. Even those whose native garb it is do not always find it pleasant, and many a time on a snowy east wind day in October the writer has seen *through the glass* one of the best known veteran stalkers of Scotland with his stockings pulled up over his thighs as high as they would come. He little knew he was being inspected! In most parts of Scotland a gillie and pony can be hired for two guineas a week, and it is worth all the money to meet the couple at the end of a hard day and home ten miles off and the rain coming down.

A friend of the writer's realized this fact so acutely, that he was once heard to exclaim *sotto voce* as he was setting off for a twelve-mile tramp from an outlying corrie, at about six o'clock on an October evening, in the face of wind, rain, and darkness, and over a very rough and steep ground, "Well, I would give twenty pounds to be able to go into Long's and get a pint of champagne and order a hansom." So if pony and gillie are to be had, reader, take advice and secure them, or the day may come when you will feel inclined to exceed my friend's bid!

These ponies are very sure-footed, and as soon as they have been along a track a few times they know it by heart, and every dangerous hole in it; over the very worst of tracks on the darkest nights they will bring the rider in safety, till a sudden neigh proclaims the lodge is near, and a few minutes later the lights of the house gladden the eyes. It is perhaps blowing great guns and raining cats and dogs, and even the pony's ears are lost in darkness; under such circumstances a hot tub, dinner, and cigar assume an altogether unwonted value.

These hill ponies are mostly turned out for the night either on to the hill or into a walled enclosure; the latter is much the best, as they cannot stray, and it saves a lot of time and trouble catching them each morning. Many lodges, however, have no enclosed place, and then to get them all in quickly the master pony should be caught first, and the rest will usually follow. It is curious how some one particular pony will assume the leadership of the others; but it always happens so, and even if half-a-dozen strange ponies that have never met before are turned out together, in a few hours, by some mutual understanding, one will take the lead and the rest will go wherever he shows the way.

Never on any pretence gallop these ponies, for being entirely grass-fed they are in no condition for it, and are quickly rendered broken-winded. Valets and servants going to post or sent on messages are frequent transgressors in this respect, and should always be strictly cautioned.

With regard to your own personal condition, if plenty of lawn tennis be played, and hansoms and "pints" eschewed, and hill-walking is not an unaccustomed exercise, the shooter will be fairly fit at the commencement of the season, and each day out will make him more so. The great thing in going up a long steep hill is to stop and *admire the view*, the moment nature warns that too great a strain is being placed on the pumping powers of the heart. Do not mind who is in front, or how far; do not struggle on till the heart is bumping against the ribs; do not be ashamed to sit down and rest. Many a good man out of condition has seriously injured that organ by trying to "live" with a practised walker up a severe hill. The Swiss guides have a very good maxim, and always urge you at the beginning of a long day "to start as if you never meant to get to the journey's end."

There are times when it is a matter of shot or no shot to reach a certain point before deer get past it; then you must make the best dash up-hill you can, and the heart must take its chance of hurt if the deer are to take theirs.

As to lunch, the less eaten while stalking the better; a hearty breakfast, a light lunch, and a good dinner will be best. If the weather, as is often the case in September, be very hot and sultry, whatever the temptation, do not stop at every spring and drink; resist at once, and the thirst by degrees will go away. Whiskey is most usually carried, but the writer has found nothing so well suited for a long day as a flask holding three or four glasses of good old port. The warmth and fillip it gives is much more lasting than whiskey; and at lunch save a biscuit and a glass for "five o'clock tea." Sandwich papers and any traces of luncheon should always either be stamped into the peat or thrown into water.

Whatever the stimulant with which the flask is filled, carry it in your own pocket, for it is quite extraordinary how unfortunate some gillies are, and the very best made flasks *will* come unscrewed or leak! Some stalkers carry cold tea, and any one with a penchant for this should always carry whiskey as well, so as to be able to offer a wee drappie to stalker or shepherd.

Fancy offering a highlander a sup of cold tea after he had just gralloched a " royal "! Unless indeed both master and man liked tea it would be almost an insult. The author does know of one solitary case where the double event takes place, and master and forester never take anything but cold tea, and can do as hard a day and shoot as straight as any; and when the echoes of Ben Alder ring to the report of this gentleman's rifle, it usually bodes ill for the stag. Let the shooter rejoice if his attendant be a temperance man; as a rule they will physically outstay the others, and are greatly to be desired, whether as stalkers, keepers, or gillies.

At the end of the day, if it is to be got at any farmhouse near, a glass of milk with a dash of whiskey in it is an excellent pick-me-up; then light the pipe and away home best pace you can.

With reference to lighting pipes, it will be wiser not to follow the example of most stalkers, and do this at the foot of a fifteen hundred foot hill, which he will ascend without a halt, puffing the while placidly at his black twist. Choose a better and more comfortable time, for what is pleasure to him will likely enough be exactly the reverse to his gentleman.

CHAPTER III.

PECULIARITIES OF DEER.

IT is not proposed to enter into a long account of the habits of deer and all their natural history, but to allude only to such traits as are absolutely necessary for every one to know who goes in pursuit of them. First and foremost, and it seems almost laughable to say it, deer *must* be approached in such a manner that they do not get the wind of the stalking party, that is, either directly up wind or on a side wind. It is almost impossible and quite a fluke if a shot is obtained by going down wind. The actual distance at which deer will take the wind is somewhat uncertain, but with a strong wind it is not safe to go within a mile of them, and the writer once saw deer *in a gale* take the wind of a man *and a pony* quite a mile and a half away. So keen is their sense of smell, that for fully an hour after a stalking party has passed by, they will not easily cross the tracks on account of the scent still hanging to them. Deer always move up wind when feeding, and if disturbed, whatever direction they may take at the first moment of alarm, they will eventually circle so as to meet it and run up wind. It is owing to this habit that in some forests the owners dare not venture out for days together for fear of sending their deer all over the country for the benefit of their neighbours. On certain grounds there are places in which, whatever and however the wind blows, so mysteriously does it eddy that it is an impossibility to stalk a deer—places in which no one has ever been known to get a shot; and these spots the deer know right well, and frequent with the most annoying regularity. When found in such a position, the only plan is to go through the form of making the attempt, and trust that when they move they will shift to better ground and eventually give a fair chance of a stalk. In the middle of the day deer usually lie down, and will sometimes so remain for two or three hours at a stretch, and nothing is more tiresome than passing this time about a hundred and fifty yards from them. Afraid to smoke, daring hardly to whisper, lying in a cramped position, perhaps knee-deep in peat or water, and exposed to a cold wind, the temptation to take a lying shot and put an end to the suspense becomes very great. Carefully a bead is drawn on the best stag, and it begins to look a certainty; but if the stalker knows his business he will do all he can to protest against the experiment being made, and in the end patience will reap the reward. If there is a big herd, the time will pass more quickly if the glass be cautiously brought to bear, and stock be taken of each individual stag. Count the points on each head, and determine which is really the most shootable, and then to fill up more time look them all over again and try to guess what each one is thinking of! If an easy chance is missed after all that waiting and all that spying, the shooter will certainly feel nearly as cheerful as if he had owned the second horse in the Derby and been beaten a head!

If deer are on a steep hillside, the biggest stags are usually at the bottom of the hill, and the smaller ones and hinds above them. When lying in a position like this, they will usually be looking straight down-hill, and if any wind to speak of is blowing, they will be on the sheltered side of the valley. This, of course, implies that the wind is coming over the top of the face on which they are, and then deer are nearly unapproachable. To get in up wind and from below is almost hopeless. If there are any shootable stags on the outskirts of the herd on either side, it is worth while attempting a stalk from the top of the hill, and quite to one side of them. Sometimes, on a very steep face and a strong wind blowing, it may be risked with success, and an attempt made direct down wind, it favouring the stalker by blowing so strongly as to carry his scent clean over their heads; but ninety-nine times out of a hundred it will betray his presence. Unless suspicious, or disturbed by grouse, fox, raven, &c., &c., deer rarely look up-hill, and for this reason it is always better to stalk down-hill.

When in large herds all sentinel work seems to be left to the care of the hinds, and unless alarmed the sight of neither stag or hind appears to be extraordinarily sharp. Once scared or their curiosity aroused by suspicion they will rarely rest till satisfied, and if only just the top of a cap has been detected, they will quickly bring their sense of smell into play by making a detour round the suspicious object till they get the wind of it.

In crawling up to a large herd, creep as cautiously as one may, it is sometimes impossible to prevent a hind seeing the top of a cap. Then watch her. Up goes her head, and for a time she and you indulge in a right good staring match. She cannot see as much as would include the tip of your nose. Will she or will she not make it out? Presently she puts her head down and takes a few bites of grass, and you think the day is won; but suddenly up it goes again, so quickly and so directly fixed on you that it seems a ruse on her part to ensure your detection. With a slow stately step, though withal somewhat "peacocky," she begins to come round you into the wind. The beginning of the end draws near. You know that if she continues her course she *must* detect you, and you lie flat and still, and hope against hope. Suddenly she has it, and with a loud bark of alarm she warns the rest and off they all go.

At times a hind will walk right up to the suspicious object, and in such a case suspense is soon over.

Deer will invariably endeavour to satisfy themselves of what they are running away from, and prefer rather to face a danger they have already ascertained the worst of, than confront one they have not thoroughly examined and satisfied themselves about. It is for this reason so many deer drives go wrong. They will fly before the drivers direct to the rifle-boxes, but an eddy of the wind, a cap shown, a shot fired too soon will turn them all into the faces of the drivers, through whom they will charge in spite of yells, waving caps, upheld arms, and sticks hurled at them, rather than face the hidden but half-detected danger in front.

Deer startled early in the day will be apt to shift their ground much further, and even when settled again be far more restless, than those disturbed at feeding-time in the afternoon. On a fine calm day they will not move nearly so far as on a cold day, with half a gale blowing. Indeed, in a high wind deer play the most fanciful tricks, and will start suddenly, and of their own accord, and dash off full tilt, and go a mile or two for no reason at all. On such days, unless the wind is exactly right for the ground to be stalked, it is far wiser to stay at home and shoot grouse or rabbits, or go fishing, or write letters, or sleep by the smoking-room fire; in short, do anything but go into the forest, where your presence will be certain to do more harm than good, by sending the deer far and wide.

In fine warm weather stags will mostly be on the very highest hills, and on wet, cold, stormy days on lower ground. They are always sharply observant of other creatures: grouse, ptarmigan, hares, ravens, and foxes, any of these, if they have been disturbed by man will tell them at once of danger, although if either one or the other move about simply for their own pleasure or convenience, they are allowed to pass by totally unheeded.

In stalking on ground that is not cleared, sheep will give deer the alarm at once, and if during a stalk sheep be met with, there is nothing for it but to stop quite still, and then gradually to sink down and let them look till they are tired of it, when they will usually feed quietly away. If a sheep is startled and runs, the stalk is almost certainly spoilt; for the chances are the moment one begins to run, others will see him and start off also; these alarm more, until in a few minutes three or four hundred sheep may be seen running up the corrie as if twenty collies were at their heels. Curious and pretty even as the sight may be, it is hardly appreciated when deer are in front, for it means good-bye to them. Therefore, however troublesome it may be, spare no pains to pass by sheep without making them run, and it is rarely but that patience will accomplish this. Now and then it will happen that having started on a stalk, a few hinds may be found in some dip of the ground, and directly in the road to the quarry, and round which it is impossible to creep without being seen. If they are not in view of the stag pursued, they may perhaps be moved sufficiently far out of the way to let you pass, without alarming them very much, either by a low whistle, or by showing the top of a stick, and waving it gently, but more often than not they will head straight for the deer you are after and take them away also.

CHAPTER IV.

THE STALK—THE SHOT.

WE will now suppose it to be a nice fine day, and everything ready for a start from the lodge. Be sure that cartridges, coat, lunch, flask, pipe and 'bacca are all with you, for in parts of the Highlands it is thought to bring bad luck to turn back for anything after having once made a start, and to do this will put some stalkers quite out of heart for the day. What nonsense! is the natural exclamation, but all the same, should the stalker be a believer in this superstition, on no account balk him. He certainly will not confess offhand to this feeling; he may go a whole season and never mention it, although plenty of articles be forgotten and he sent back for them, but one day when something extra bad has happened to interfere with the sport, he will perhaps quietly confide in you. Therefore once possessed of the knowledge of this fetish on his part, if lunch or tobacco is found missing a short distance from home, why go on boldly without it. The stalker will not have forgotten either one or the other as far as he is concerned, and will be proud to give you a bite, or a pipe of his black cavendish. The mere fact of his being a believer in this sort of bad luck is apt to make him rash and nervous, and even if all goes well with the stalk and the shooter miss, it will all be put down to that "dommed turning back." The feeling is stronger, but the same as may have been experienced by some of my readers if they are whist-players. There are times when one cuts into a rubber feeling certain to lose it, and how often does success follow such a presentiment?

At last being fairly under weigh, an hour or so on pony-back or on foot will bring you to the spying-stone, or spot from which it is customary to take the first spy of the ground to be stalked. It is by no means easy to search a corrie properly with the glass. If there is but a gentle breeze, the walking-stick planted firmly in the earth will give sufficient support to keep the glass steady. The best spying position is to lie nearly flat on the back, with a stone or tussock of grass to rest the shoulders against; then drawing up the knees, hold the glass firmly against the left knee, and you will be able to hold it perfectly steady in a high wind. Practice alone will make an adept in "picking up" deer, but *absolute immovability* of the glass is the first thing to ensure success. If deer are lying quite still in broken ground the novice may often have the exact spot pointed out to him, and yet be quite unable to find them. Spying is usually a moist process, and some who fear rheumatism and dislike sitting on wet moss, fasten a small square of mackintosh to their coats, and on this they can sit while spying, and put it into their pocket when the spy is over; if it is not fastened to the coat it will almost surely be left behind them

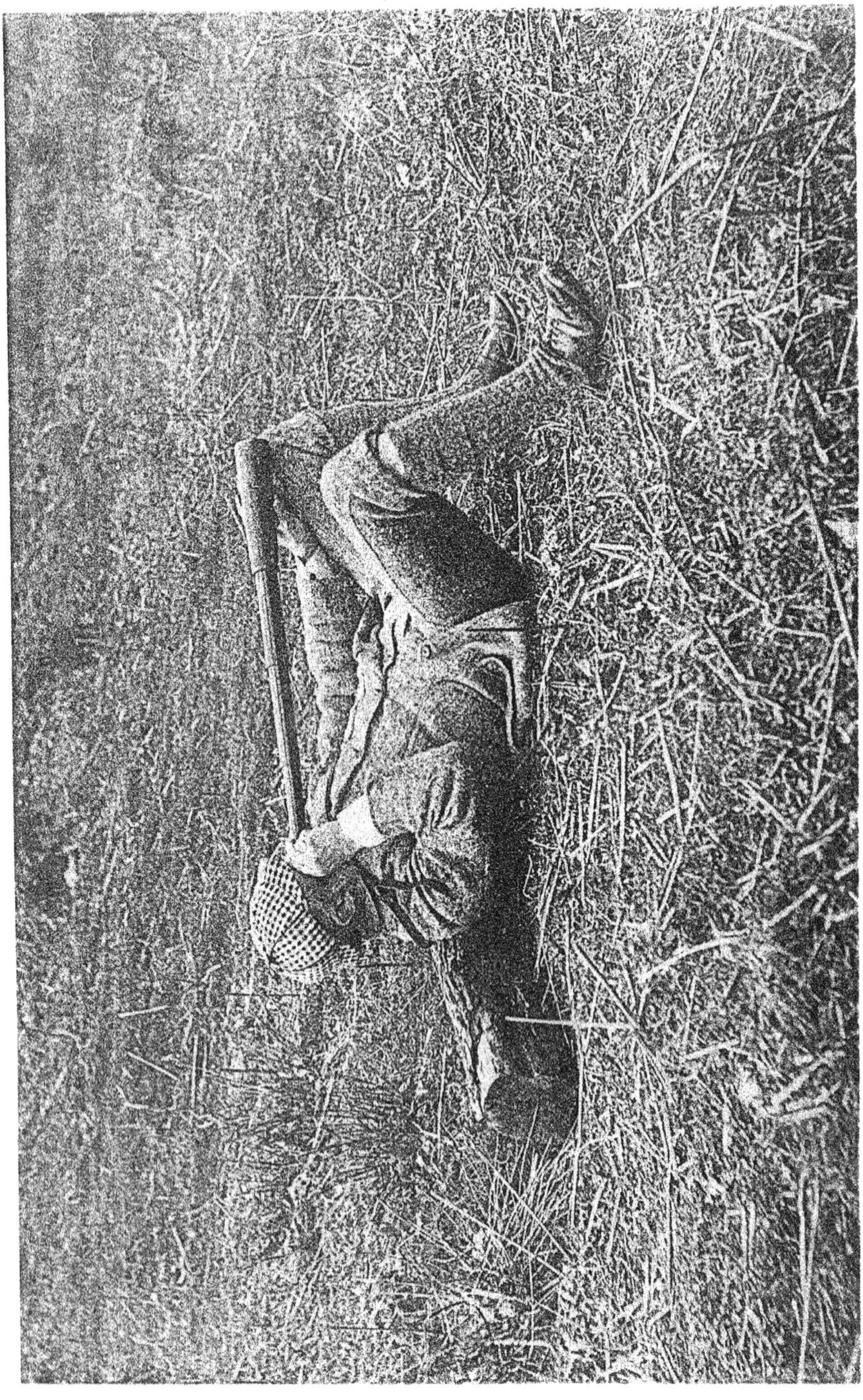

first time deer are found and plans for stalking them discussed.

In using the spy-glass, if the sun is shining at your back, and you are spying straight down-hill, be careful not to take the glass from the eye and hold it so that the sun's rays pass through it; should this precaution be neglected the deer will be treated to a regular Crystal Palace display of fireworks which they will not stay long to admire. The writer has never heard of this matter being mentioned or noticed, but it was vividly brought to his observation by the loss of a shot at several good stags. It had been agreed over-night that we should try and get at some deer in a corrie where the stalking was very difficult, and where there were usually some extra good stags. One of us was to stalk and the other was to post himself in a pass for which they usually made when disturbed. We tossed for choice, and it fell to my lot to proceed to the pass. There was a high steep hill between the stalking party and this pass. After a long wait we saw a great lot of deer come over the top of this hill, and we knew that the stalk had failed. They came right over the top, not much alarmed, and wended their way to the foot; there they halted for about a quarter of an hour, and then began quietly to come towards our pass. We had already picked out the two best stags, and a good shot seemed certain, but suddenly, and when about three hundred yards off our hiding-place, the whole lot turned to the right-about and made off full tilt, evidently much alarmed. We were certain they could not have seen us or got our wind, and, much puzzled, turned round and looked behind us, when brilliant flashes of fire proceeding from the sky-line of the hill greeted our eyes. Bringing the glasses to bear, we found they came from the stalking party, who, having followed the deer up the hill, had sat down and taken a spy at the disturbed herd, and having seen enough, were sitting still with their glasses over their shoulders, and the sun's rays, passing directly through the telescope, caused the brilliant coruscations we beheld, and which had scared the deer so much.

Having found deer, simply put yourself in your stalker's hands; for without a most intimate acquaintance with the ground—a knowledge which is only acquired by being on it daily for many months, if not years—it is almost impossible to manage the stalk alone. After some experience you may have the satisfaction of doing the last two or three hundred yards, and even in that short distance you often blunder and have to retreat and crawl back again and make a fresh start; perhaps compelled to do this twice or thrice, and so lose much valuable time; whereas, if it had been left to the stalker, he would, from his better knowledge of the ground, have gone straight in without a halt. A few minutes often makes all the difference between an easy shot and a difficult one, or perhaps no shot at all. In crawling or creeping up-hill or on level ground, always advance head first; but in going down-hill in any position let your feet go first. In a very flat creep, punt yourself along with the elbows, and be careful to keep the legs flat, for somehow or other the feet have a tendency to throw themselves up above the level of the head. Keep close to the stalker, and be *sure* and keep as *low as he does*. One who understands his work will often only be an inch or two out of sight of his quarry, and it is unfair, and enough to make him think unutterable things, if, keeping a few inches higher than he is, you let the deer into the secret just at the end of the stalk. Few things can be more disheartening or trying to his temper than for him to find all the trouble he has taken to get his gentleman a shot has been wasted through carelessness. I remember hearing of the quiet sarcasm of a stalker, who, just at the end of a very long creep, had seen the deer put away by his gentleman.

"Why, what on earth could have put them away?" exclaimed the disappointed sportsman. Gravely to him replied the stalker, who had been advancing *flat on his stomach*, while the gentleman had been crawling on his *hands and knees*, "Why, you was just waalking when I was craaling."

We will take it for granted that the shooter has had "stag fever," and is well over it, or perhaps nature has made him altogether superior to such a malady. But if he have not escaped it—and if there are two novices together it is as catching as measles—the disease must run its course; advice will not cure, *neither will whiskey;* but after a course of downright bad misses the foresight of your rifle will by degrees cease to wobble round and round. The eye will clearly see that there *is* a stag within a hundred yards, and the brain begin to tell that it will be better to keep the sight steady if you wish to taste one of his haunches instead of sending him off to give a treat to a neighbour. In stalking on sheep ground, and as far as deer go, it is quite legitimate to use the old Highlander's prayer, "Oh, Lard, tak' everything from everybody and gie it a' to me'" In getting near deer never come *over* a boulder or a hillock, but always creep *round* it. It is a sign of bad stalking if the stalker is continually stopping dead and suddenly bobbing down. Walking too fast is apt to produce this style, for in going at a great pace with deer in front it becomes almost impossible for the eye to guard three or four hundred yards on either side; the country is opened up *too quickly*, and frequently the deer get a good look at you before they themselves are seen.

And now for the critical and exciting moment of taking the shot. For two hours, perhaps for three or four, or longer even, has the sportsman walked, run, crawled, crept, and waited, and done all he could to outwit his quarry, and the next few minutes will decide whether all his exertion and his trouble has been taken in vain. Small wonder that anxiety for the result should take possession of him. If the stag is standing still and broadside on, the best plan is to put the rifle sights on the inside of his fore-leg, bring them very slowly up the leg till it joins the body, and then when you "see brown" press, or rather squeeze the trigger gently. This was the receipt of the late Colonel Campbell of Monzie, than whom there was no one in all Scotland more able to give good advice on such a matter. The probabilities are that in every shot the bullet will strike a little higher than the exact spot

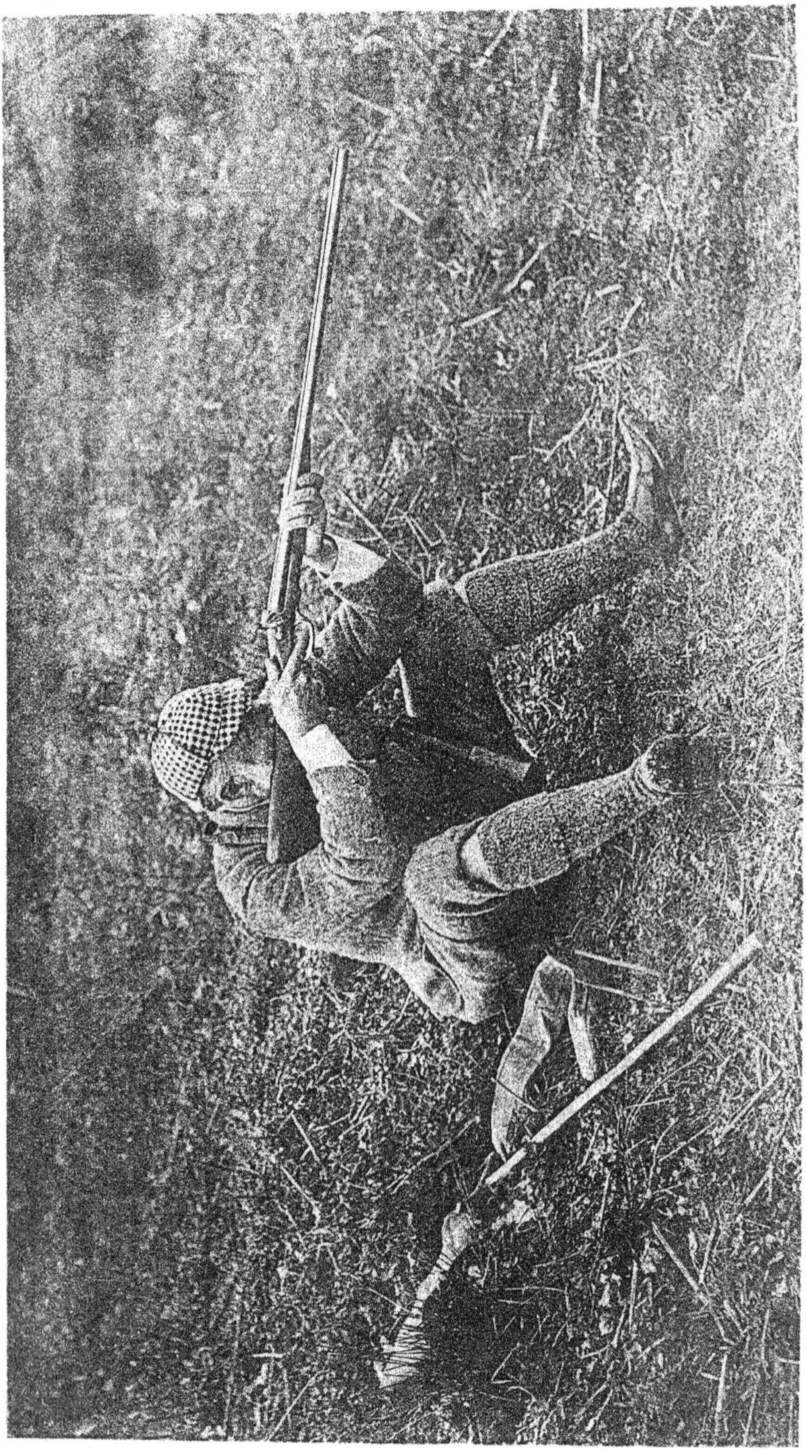

THE SHOT.

aimed at; whether a few inches to the right or left matters not, it will be equally fatal. Do not fire at deer standing end on or facing you; even if they appear alarmed, wait quietly, and they will usually give a fair chance. In shooting down-hill sit up and plant the heels firmly in the ground, resting both the elbows on the thighs; in shooting up-hill seek for a tussock or a big stone round which to push the rifle, and lie flat behind it, but do not on any account fire off the shoulder as if shooting at a cock grouse. Especially do not sit up and fire off the shoulder if it is an up-hill shot; for you will be so inclined to fall backwards that it becomes impossible to hold the rifle steady. Crawl in and get a rest: do this if even there are a hundred eyes apparently all looking at you; the cap is all they can see, and if that is of a good colour, and moves slowly, deer will stay staring at it and trying to make out what it is, and before they have done that a shot can generally be taken. In firing at moving deer practice alone will teach how far to hold in front. In the event of the too frequent miss, note if the deer was trotting slowly or fast, or galloping best pace, and always ask the stalker where the bullet struck, and, profiting by the observation, the next time a like chance presents it will most likely end in a kill. As a rule shoot *right at* a walking deer; the bullet goes up so quickly from the express rifle, that even if it strikes an inch or two behind the heart it is fatal. At a deer trotting slowly fire at the point of the shoulder, but if he be trotting very fast, just see daylight in front of him and then pull; but for a deer *galloping* as fast as he can, from two to three feet may be "borrowed." In a gale a good allowance must be made for windage if shooting across wind. A very good rifle shot, and most skilful stalker, has assured me that in a shot of this sort—that is, in a gale—and the deer standing head down wind and broadside on, it is common to aim at the haunches and hit in the heart! Whether in up-hill or down-hill shots with the express rifle, there need hardly be any variation made in the sight taken; it will make the shot more certain, however, if in a down-hill shot the aim is a little beneath the heart, and in an up-hill one a little over it. The foregoing remarks are "good" for shots at distances varying from eighty to one hundred and twenty yards; at longer ranges they would require greater allowances to be made. If making a long run up, and only getting within shot at the moment of stopping, and you are panting with the exertion, the rifle will be held more steadily if you aim and fire in the few seconds between exhaling and again inhaling. Do not attempt very long shots; any stag over two hundred yards should always be waited on for hours on the chance of getting closer. If the stag is standing well and the light good, it *should* be killed at that distance, but it is also uncommonly often missed. Nothing but darkness coming on, or the certainty of getting no nearer, should justify a shot at any deer over this distance, for even if a hit is made it is almost sure to be only a wound, which the deer will carry off with him, suffer from for weeks and weeks, and eventually die of.

Having missed with the right barrel do not empty the

left in a hurry; take time to steady yourself, and then seize the first fair chance; it will usually present itself, and if it does not it is almost better to refrain from firing at all, for it is of very little use to do so at deer running away end on. Should you, however, in the excitement of the moment be unable to resist, then pitch the rifle-sight quickly in the centre of his horns and directly above the crown of the head, and pull the trigger as if taking a snap shot with a gun. A shot of this sort rarely comes off, but if it does the deer is almost certainly killed dead; if it fails, the deer escapes unhurt, and the risk of haunching him is reduced to a minimum. If both barrels are emptied in vain, then in the name of all that is sportsman-like do not be persuaded to sit down and open fire at random, and as fast as it is possible to blaze away. Do not "brown" them; it would cause a shudder to hear of a covey of birds being so served, and it is a thousand times worse to treat a herd of deer like this! Not once in fifty times is a *good* stag bagged by such a process; when anything is bagged at all, a calf or a pricket is more often the reward of the folly; a poor little beast which one is ashamed to mention in the smoking-room after dinner, and which a good-natured stalker will usually offer to bury, and whose epitaph is, "We will just say no more about it and try for a better ane." Having already missed with both barrels, if six or eight more cartridges are discharged at fast vanishing deer, what with the noise of the reports, the whistling of the bullets, and the "smacking" they make as they strike on rock or peat, it will give the flying herd such a scare that they do not forget it for many days; they will desert that part of the ground and perhaps be driven quite away. There are young stalkers, bloodthirsty, excitable, and keen, who will maybe try and preach to the contrary. They have in all probability taken their gentleman up well; procured him a good and easy shot; and as first one barrel then the other is emptied in vain, they grow frantic and long to see a beast roll on the heather. So it is, " Now, sir, again!" and as you open the rifle-breech, two fresh cartridges are thrust in, and crack! crack! they go, the deer two hundred and fifty yards away, and no result. These are hurriedly followed by two more, and again the hills echo to the reports of the wasted cartridges. The writer has known this fusillade kept up till deer were fully five hundred yards away!

After missing with both barrels keep as much concealed and as still as possible, but load again instantly in case the deer take a circle, which they will sometimes do, and thereby offer *really* good and easy second chances. If they continue their straight-away course, sit still and blame the rifle, the deer, or the stalker, or the light, and generally try and recover as quickly as maybe from the depressing effects of the miss.

A gentleman who had distinguished himself by a series of brilliant misses, on the last of these sad misfortunes somewhat feebly remarked to his stalker, "Well, Donald, whose fault was it that time?" and received for reply, "Well, he wasn't more than a hundred yards, and it's not my fault you missed him; and it wasn't the fault of the stag, for he stood still

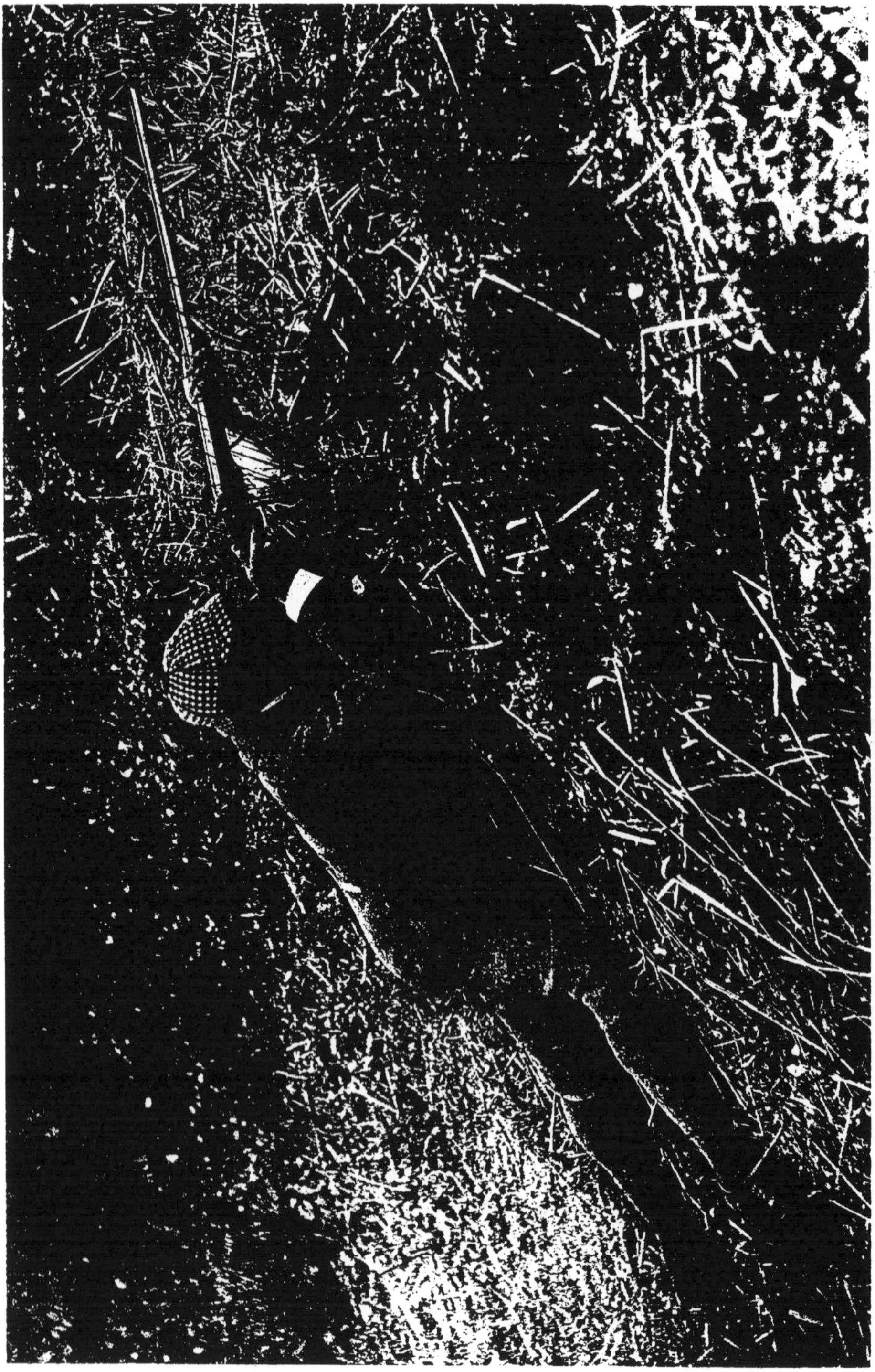

enough; and it's not the fault of the rifle, for I ken well it's a right good one, so I'll just leave it to you to think it over and find out whose fault it was."

This was all said in such a very respectful and matter-of-fact way, and as if the stalker himself was puzzled, and thought there might be some solution of the question other than the only one his logic had left possible, that it would have been churlish to take offence, and in a few moments the shooter was laughing heartily, and Donald and he were drinking better luck next time.

When lying flat and firing over a tussock, do not fire through long grass; it is impossible to get a proper sight if there are a lot of the long yellow blades of grass peculiar to the hills, waving about in front of the fore sight. Novices will, however, attempt to do so for fear of being seen if they raise themselves any higher; but a very few inches will clear the grass, and if the rise be made very slowly on one elbow, detection rarely ensues. It is as well to carry a few cartridges in your own pocket, in addition to the supply the stalker will have with him, for it is possible to become parted for a short distance. Do not cock the rifle till expecting to shoot; the triggers are usually set so light, and the sight of deer only three hundred yards off is so apt unconsciously to make the finger place itself on the trigger, that accidents will happen, and to say nothing of any danger, such a catastrophe as the letting off a barrel by accident will surely spoil your sport. Now and then it will occur that during a long wait for deer to rise, an irresistible desire comes to choke, or cough, or sneeze. A sup of water may put matters right if there is any handy, if not, then bury nose and mouth in the peat and explode therein; no matter if you come up looking like a Christy minstrel, it will wash off or dry off very quickly.

On a very still day doubts frequently arise as to which way the currents of air are moving. If a finger be wetted and held up, one can usually feel and see which side is drying first and is coldest; or a bit of cotton grass dropped from the hand, or if there is none near, a bit of fluff picked off your coat will answer the purpose equally well.

If the ground or the deer should so favour, that you find yourself from thirty to fifty yards from them, *then* is the time all your wits will be wanted to avoid a miss, for, strange as it may read, there are every year a great number of misses made at these very close quarters.

The tendency of all express rifles is to throw the bullet very high in the first fifty yards of its flight. The rifle will be sighted for a hundred yards, and if this sight is used for a shot at forty yards, it will usually put the ball over the deer. Almost every one who has been after them much will have sad recollections of missing shots of this description—shots which have been delivered with the greatest confidence, and feeling certain that the trigger had but to be pressed to ensure possession of the prize; and the greater the feeling of confidence, the greater the annoyance and vexation at missing. These are the shots that are thought of with wonder and regret for weeks, perhaps months, afterwards. There are two ways of taking these shots at close quarters. Either aim straight at the heart, and be *very* careful to take the sight *extremely* fine, much finer than if firing a shot at a hundred yards or thereabouts; or take the sight as if firing at that distance, but keep it just on the *outline* of the deer, *directly under the heart.*

One of these two shots must be tried; a little practise with the rifle will soon tell which comes the easiest and most natural. The writer, for his part, prefers the last mentioned method. Directly a beast drops to shot, no matter whether near or far off, run up to him at once, and as fast as possible. If the ball has gone high and just grazed the spine without breaking it, the shock will cause a deer to lie helpless for a few minutes, but if the shooter be not up to him at once, he will quickly recover and be gone. In any case get up to him as fast as you can; nothing is more vexatious than to wound a stag, and then to see him rise and trot away while the pursuers are yet a good way off. He will be pretty sure to give a poor second chance, and you are probably so disconcerted by his unexpected resurrection and evident strength, that a hurried shot is followed by a miss.

Now and then it happens, if stalking near the march, that when spying, the glass will wander across it to explore Naboth's vineyard, and in so doing will discover Naboth himself in pursuit of his deer. In this case, if he has not seen you first, it is as well to sit down and watch his proceedings for a while. If there are deer in front of him, it is possible that his misfortune may become your good luck, for any mistake on his part may send the deer to you. The writer remembers a bit of friendly chaff which occurred to himself in this very way. He had been waiting near his march for nearly an hour at a little over one hundred yards from some deer that were lying down, and seemingly thoroughly bent on resting a considerable time longer. To pass the time he was trying to make a rough sketch on an old envelope of the shooting lodge in the distance, and trusting the stalker to watch the deer and tell him of any movement on their part. Suddenly, without a moment's warning, there is whispered " Quick, sir, they are all off ! " and snatching up the rifle, there was nothing to be seen but some retreating heads, and taking a hasty sight between a pair of good horns, the trigger was pressed and the deer clean missed. It certainly was not a miss to "greet" over, and no more was said about it, though we speculated a good deal as to what put them so suddenly away.

A day or two afterwards one of our pony men brought my stalker a message from Naboth's stalker, to say " he'd best tell his master to get some straight powder," and on further inquiry we found our neighbours had been about a mile off watching our performance, and hoping we should send the deer to them. This, however, had not happened, and so, comforting ourselves with this knowledge, we tried to feel as little nettled as possible at the remark. My stalker, however, could not swallow the chaff at all; it was always on his mind, and for days after, whenever he went near the march, his glass was incessantly directed across it, in the hopes of getting his revenge. About a week later, happening to be on the same ground again, but quite early in the morning, we turned our glasses on the path by which our neighbours would come if they were to be out that day, and there sure enough we saw them advancing. On examining the intervening ground we found a good stag, some smaller ones, and a lot of hinds with him. Of course the approaching party had seen them also, and right well did their man take his gentleman up. He had a quiet standing broadside shot, and missed; then another puff of smoke was visible through the glass, and another miss, and their deer were heading full tilt towards us. A hasty shift of ground, about three hundred yards to our right, brings us into position; a wait of a few minutes, and past us they all come, the hinds showing the way, and the big stag comes last but one. We know the glasses of the other party are on them, so taking the greatest care, I press the trigger, and as the smoke clears, there he lies stone dead. Turning round I find my stalker dancing as near to a breakdown as any Highlander dare when "on business," but he is smiling pleasantly and vowing loudly that we are more than quits with the noble earl who was reported to have sent us the straight powder message!

It is always most amusing to watch through the glass the stalking of another party—their creeping and crawling appears so comical, and they are so perfectly unconscious of being watched. N.B.—Engaged couples and honeymooners will do well to bear this in mind if they are wandering in the vicinity of deer forests!

There is usually a mutual understanding known as "stalker's law" between forests where the marches join, and that is, that it is permissible to either party, finding deer on his own ground, but so close to the march that they are not stalkable except by crossing it, to come over on to his neighbour's ground sufficiently far to hide his cap whilst crawling on his hands and knees. Between some forests there is a further understanding, that a wounded deer may be followed across the march. The better and more usual plan, however, is to send a letter to the occupier of the adjoining ground, and inform him that a wounded deer has been sent to him, and ask that his foresters be told to keep a look out for it. If the march be crossed in pursuit of a wounded deer it is almost sure to spoil the sport of any other party that is out on the adjoining beat; also, in the event of the wind blowing strongly from the *backs* of the search party, they will be very liable to move a lot of deer, which on being disturbed will run up wind and right on to the ground where the deer was wounded. With a wind like this, some not over-nice foresters will see a deer wounded and take over the march with vast satisfaction; and when in pursuit they will take no pains to go quietly, or to keep themselves as much as maybe out of sight, well knowing that every deer they move will head up wind direct on to their own ground, and then if it holds in the same quarter till next morning, there will be a good chance at some of their neighbour's deer the next day. It goes without saying that most stalkers will find extra pleasure in killing a good stag coming from Naboth's vineyard, and the ground that is "over the march" is always Naboth's, no matter what the actual facts of the case may be.

It must be mentioned, that the illustrations of "an uphill shot" and a "downhill shot" have both been purposely photographed with the sole view of showing the best and most comfortable positions in which to take them. On actual service there would of course be some further cover for the shooter, either of rock, hillock, heather, or bracken, but it was necessary to omit these in order to show clearly what was intended.

CHAPTER V.

WOUNDED DEER — DEER-HOUNDS AND COLLIES — WEIGHTS OF DEER—"FLESH, FISH, AND FOWL"— THE GRALLOCH.

WHEN a deer is hit and recovers himself, remain hidden and keep perfectly still; turn the glass on to him quickly and ascertain where he is struck, and watch him closely. Wherever he be wounded, it is almost certain he will make for water, and having found it, will then seek a hole in which to lie down and hide. If the ground serves, and he does not become unsighted, and you can see him do this, then to the larder he should go, for he is usually an easy stalk when in such a sorry plight.

If he goes out of sight over a ridge and does not again appear beyond it, get up to the place where he disappeared, and then proceed exactly as if he were lying in front of you; if he is not going away to either side he may be lying dead, and if not, a careful spy will mostly find him. It is extraordinary how closely a badly-wounded deer will lie, and how cleverly and in how small a hole he will conceal himself. When the surface is broken by precipitous gullies and watercourses filled with old heather and bracken, he will lie so closely that he may easily be passed by; especially will he lie extra close if he has been wounded some days previously; therefore, if he has vanished in such sort of ground every bit of it must be thoroughly searched, and often he will start to life within a few yards. Occasionally it happens that deer unsight you the moment the shot is delivered, and then run as fast as may be to some spot commanding a view of the flying herd. If the stag shot at is not with them, return at once to the place they bolted from, and follow the tracks carefully, and he will more often than not be found lying dead, or so badly hurt as to be incapable of flight. The ability to tell almost at a glance whether the stag fired at is with a vanishing herd, varies to a great degree even among old and experienced foresters, but to a novice it is almost a hopeless task. It is difficult even if a deer with some marked peculiarity has been shot at, as, for instance, one with an oddly-shaped horn, or "mouse-coloured," or one that has just been rolling in peat, and is black; but without something of this sort to mark him it becomes well-nigh impossible for a novice to "spot" him amidst even only a dozen others. A stag not very severely wounded, if he detects your approach, will rarely rest again till he has gone a great distance, and rendered pursuit almost useless.

If a stag be struck in such a way that he cannot rise, and is yet very strong and full of life, especially if he is sitting up, and has the full use of his fore-legs, be very careful how an approach within reach of his horns be made, for he will stab viciously with them, and with a half-rush, half-push make a furious effort to avenge himself.

Only once have I seen a wounded deer actually charge. He was hit high up in the back (as it afterwards turned out, the spine was "chipped" but not broken), and running up to give the *coup de grâce*, I plunged up to my hips in some soft ground when about fifteen yards off. Turning to extricate myself, a yell from the stalker warned me only just in time to put in a snap shot; he had regained his legs, and was coming full tilt for his destroyer, and he fell with his nose almost touching me.

As to the use of dogs, some prefer deer-hounds, some collies, and others again prohibit their use altogether. The deer-hound is certainly a far more beautiful dog to look at than the collie—he is fiercer of aspect, and there is a something in the great long head, the wide-opening jaws, far-seeing eyes, and lengthy, wiry body that seems in harmony with the wildness of the scenery and the sport. To see a good dog slipped at a deer is indeed a sight to remember. To watch him overtake and place himself alongside of a galloping stag, and then to see him seize the foreleg; roll the stag over; shift his hold in a moment and fix his teeth in the throat, and kill quickly, is indeed a fine spectacle. Young deer-hounds are very apt to be rash, and having brought the deer to bay, will go in and try to pull it down and kill for themselves; in this manner many a good hound has met his death, for if the hound be not very fast, before the quarry be brought to bay, he will usually have reached water, and taken up his position in a torrent, with his hind quarters safe from attack, and where the stream runs deep and swift in front of him. A hound attacking in such a position is at a great disadvantage, and even if not mortally wounded is pretty certain to be sharply hurt. The writer remembers a very fine deer-hound being slipped at a wounded stag late one evening in October; both were soon lost to sight in the twilight, and though sought for patiently, and till a late hour that night, and all the day following, and for many a day after, neither dog nor stag were ever heard of more, and this though a large reward was offered for the dog dead or alive. Probably pursued and pursuer rolled together over some precipice and were dashed to pieces by the fall, and the foxes, eagles, and ravens soon picked their bones.

The collie, though not such a taking-looking dog as the deer-hound, is usually quite as clever, and has the great advantage of being more under control. I have stalked with two collies so perfectly under command that no leash was required—their master could put them down at any period of a stalk by a move of his hand, and there they would lie, no matter what went on in front, till they were signalled to rejoin the party; so well in hand were they, that one could be shown a wounded deer, *both seeing it*, and only one sent after it, the other dog lying motionless and watching the chase; but whichever was sent was wonderfully quick and sure, and held the bay in a beautiful manner. If by any chance the deer outwitted the first dog, then the second one was sent off, and rarely unsuccessfully.

Many gentlemen like to see their dogs pull down a

deer and kill gallantly. Numbers of valuable dogs are, however, mortally wounded in doing this, and the writer is inclined to the opinion that they should not be urged to go in at a stag; their duty should rather be to run them to bay, and then as long as the deer stands still on the defensive, they should bark and pretend to attack; but if the deer begins to move off, then they should take a nip at his hind quarters, which instantly brings him to the defensive again, and so they should hold him at bay till the rifle comes up and puts an end to it. It is hardly possible to write of these things without recalling Ansdell's splendid paintings and Col. Crealock's clever sketches, and it would be superfluous to attempt their description when these scenes have been brought in such spirited and realistic manner to the eyes of all.

In shooting at deer at bay great care must be taken that the neck of the deer and the dog are not in the same line; with an active dog bounding about in front of the deer's head, one will often be obliged to wait some minutes before a safe shot can be delivered, therefore be in no hurry to shoot; for you would never forgive yourself, and never be forgiven, if you killed the dog. Those gentlemen who altogether prohibit the use of dogs in their forests, do so on the ground that when one is slipped at a deer the rest of the herd are so much frightened and scared, and are sent so far afield, that even though the wounded one be secured, more harm is done to the forest than will compensate for the haunches put into the larder. Should a dog be outwitted by a wounded stag and miss him, he may follow the unwounded ones for miles, and in so doing disturb a very large area of ground, both during the pursuit and on the return journey home, for he will sometimes be away for hours at a stretch and altogether lose his master.

One of the last shots I had this season afforded a very pretty, but most annoying display of the cunning of a stag hard pressed. We had been out all day without getting a shot, and found ourselves about half-past five nearly three hundred yards off a lot of stags. The ground was very flat; to get nearer was impossible, and we discussed whether such a long shot should be taken, hoping all the time that they would feed towards us; this, however, they did not do, and knowing it was my only chance that day, and a good stag standing well out, I took the shot, and smashed his fore-leg near the shoulder. The dog was slipped, or rather ordered to go in pursuit, for he was one of the collies previously alluded to, and as bad luck would have it, that day we had but the one dog with us. The deer were heading as hard as they could to a burn with high and steep banks; as they came to it the good dog was already close on them, and as they disappeared into it we expected to hear the bay, and looking on the stag as our own, began to run up. To our dismay, as they came again into sight after crossing the burn, we saw the dog dashing on after the herd and the wounded one not with them; he had cleverly hidden himself in the burn while the dog passed by, he most unluckily going between the wounded stag and the wind. As soon as the dog was well away after the others the stricken deer jumped up and was off before we were in shot, and having seen us running up, we were speedily unsighted. We followed for a long way but could see no more of him, and tramped home ten miles in the dark abusing our bad luck, for the dog must have passed within a few yards of his hiding-place: it was just simply real bad luck, and no fault of his.

The weight of deer varies in different forests according to food and climate: in some it ranges from fourteen to twenty-one stone, and in others from thirteen to seventeen; but they vary a stone more or less on the average according to the weather in the spring. The one just passed (1885) was in many parts of Scotland unusually late and cold, and on the high grounds of Perthshire, Forfarshire, and Aberdeenshire many feet of snow fell in May, and laid for a considerable time, stopping the growth of the grass and making it quite a month late in sprouting. In forests thus visited the deer killed in the following autumn scaled fully a stone less on the average than they would do in fine and open spring times. Where there is plenty of wood on the low grounds for deer to shelter in during the severity of the winter, they grow much heavier than in forests where there is no such protection. In the Duke of Hamilton's forests in the Isle of Arran it is not rare to kill deer of twenty-five and even twenty-seven stone; in most forests, however, any stag between seventeen and twenty-one stone is reckoned a real good one.

The best stags and the best hinds always being killed

does much to spoil the breeding of large deer. I admit it may be an error to advance the proposition that there are far too many calves and hinds in most forests; but their name is legion. If there are an excessive quantity, the numbers in excess of what there should be, will deprive the stags and strong hinds of a great quantity of grass they would otherwise consume, and no animal can arrive at perfection without easy, good, and plentiful feeding. Whether right or wrong in this matter, there can be no dispute that "royals" and very heavy stags are becoming scarcer each year, and this also in spite of the "sanctuary" most forests possess, and which till the end of September is the fixed abode of the best stags.

The killing of young stags also contributes largely to the falling off in size, for it may be taken for granted that if a hundred deer be shot in a forest during the season, *at least forty of them will be four-year-old deer*, which if spared for another two years would grow into fine heavy beasts, with large heads. If every stag were left to attain his six years it is still very doubtful if they would *all* become royals. In English parks those so left usually do show the twelve points at that age, but with the wild red deer there is nothing certain known on the subject. The most experienced foresters differ on the matter, many maintaining that a certain number of stags are "born royals" and will attain to that honour if left to live long enough, while others, even if spared for eight or ten years, will never arrive at the dignity: be this as it may, there cannot be a doubt that every four-year-old stag, spared for another two years, will have a much heavier body and finer and larger horns than if killed earlier. In some parts of the Highlands, so great is the admiration of the foresters for a royal, that they will approach the dead monarch with uncovered heads! The extraordinary rapid growth of the horn is one of the most remarkable features of stag life. Usually shed some time in the month of March, by the end of July they are again fully grown, though still covered with velvet. In about four months a heavy healthy stag will shoot out some seventy inches of horns—or fully four inches a week!

"That's the crop that thrives best in these parts," a forester once sadly observed to me, the while turning his eyes woefully from his own small crop of ungrown oats to a herd of deer we had been looking at one August day. During August, or the early part of September—depending entirely on the clemency or reverse of the season,—the velvet will be shed and the horns appear in all their rough and wild-shaped beauty.

The engraving annexed is the head of a wild red deer, shot in Lord Dunmore's forest in Harris, by my old friend, the late Herbert Wood of Raasay. A grand head and a fourteen pointer: if his lordship has many like this one to be seen in his forest he is indeed a lucky man; but the head is so unusually large for that part of Scotland, that I cannot help thinking this stag must have been up to a trick or two, and knew where he could go to get good and plenteous food all the winter. There is, however, no reason why every forest in Scotland should not annually produce a dozen

A FOURTEEN-POINTER

or so as good, if it be carefully shot, solely with a view to quality and not quantity. As matters stand at present, in many forests not a single Royal is bagged the whole season, and there are not many that will yield three or four!

In some parts of the Highlands hind shooting commences as early as the 1st of November. Now supposing that stag shooting ceases on the 10th of October, why should not *the owner* begin to shoot hinds on the 15th? It is but a fortnight before the recognized period. At this date it is *certain* that there are plenty of very fat hinds, for in the course of ten years I have seen many shot by accident at even an earlier date, and can vouch for it that the greater number cut up into fat and good venison—much more so than if killed in January after a lot of snow and hard weather. Against this suggestion it will doubtlessly be urged that it would disturb the stags while still with the hinds. It is questionable whether it would do so more than when shooting the hinds in the winter. Granted that the stags have separated from the hinds when these latter are usually shot, yet the foresters must disturb and alarm the stags in going over the ground in quest of their consorts. The rents of deer forests are very heavy, stalking lasts but two months, and likely enough the best half of that time may be spoilt by misty weather. If the owner of a forest after an interval of a few days could at once begin hind-shooting, many, I imagine, would be glad to stay in the North till the first half of November had passed, and enjoy this sport before handing the rest of the fun over to the stalkers; also with the prospect of this extra time of sport in front of him, he would be more apt to spare his four-year-old stags, and give them a chance of filling out.

In the two counties of Argyle and Inverness only, and leaving Mr. Winans out of the calculation, there are a dozen deer forests which let at a sum total of £25,000!—an average of over £2000 a year each. For practically two months' sport, a rental of £250 a week, or over £40 a day, is paid. This sum does not include the attendant expenses, which in some cases amount to very nearly as much again. If to this be added the consideration, that out of the two months a great number of days are wasted by bad weather, it will be seen that deer-stalking on a large scale is a most costly amusement; therefore, if any gentleman would try the suggestion I have ventured to make as to hind shooting, and it was found a good one, then the renters of forests would at least have more sport for their money. Some of these dozen forests have grouse shootings and salmon fishings also—but the bulk of the rent is paid for the stalking. In the face of this large outlay, it is yet certain, that for those who can afford the luxury it is money well spent. To say nothing of the sport obtained, and the invigorating life led, the two months passed on the hills leave behind them a sound and healthy state of mind and body with which to combat the cares and worries of the remainder of the year, and as every one knows, even the very richest cannot escape their share of these. In the expenditure of such large sums there will also be the satisfaction of knowing that, directly or indirectly, for many miles round, all the working bees of the neighbourhood will be more or less benefited. There are no co-operative stores in the Highlands: farmers, foresters, keepers, gillies, pony-men, labourers, butchers, bakers, and washerwomen, and all the hundred and one suppliers of the necessaries and comforts which go to make up the whole harmonious working of a large establishment, will each and all be gainers by the forest. The landlord also contributes his share to the widespread expenditure;—he will have the house to keep in repair, roads to mend, and fresh pony tracks to make, and generally to keep everything in good working order—a matter which will often make a big hole in his apparently large rental.

Hind shooting is by no means a sport to be despised. They are more difficult to approach than stags, but from their greater numbers, stalks and shots are plentiful, and it greatly improves one's shooting, as there is not the same anxiety to kill as the presence of a good stag gives rise to; also there is plenty of practise at running shots, without any occasion to be very down-hearted at a miss.

It is often supposed that the foresters pick off none but "yeld" or barren hinds, but it would be impossible to kill a hundred of these in any forest; and as the venison is mostly given away to all and every one living on the edge of it, the very thin, weakly hinds are seldom in much danger from the rifle. Unlike cattle, sheep, and grouse, deer are not liable to become the victims of any disease which kills them off by hundreds, and there need be no anxiety on that head.

In some forests stalking is discontinued as early as the 6th October, but the date most generally observed is the 10th of the month. It does not very much matter for a day or two, as, even if you stalk them and the glass shows they are not shootable, they can be left in peace. They do not all become poor on the same day; on the three or four days following the 10th there are still fat and good deer to be shot. If any of these days comes on a Saturday it is a good one on which to stop for the season; on the Sabbath you and yours will go to Kirk in the morning, and put an extra sovereign in the poor box, and then the afternoon will be passed in settling the smaller details of the journey south. In late and very backward seasons, like the past one (1885), deer may be safely shot a few days later; indeed, the Court Circular, which I presume is correct to a nicety, states that "on the 17th October the Duke of Connaught and Prince Henry of Battenberg went out deer-stalking," and the almost phenomenal lateness of the season would doubtlessly justify this.

With a view to improve the breed, the experiment has been tried of importing both red deer stags and hinds from English parks, where they attain great weight and grow magnificent heads—twenty, twenty-four, and even twenty-six points being not uncommon; I am not able to state the result from any personal observation, but have heard on good authority it has ended in disappointment. I have seen the reverse operation tried with success, and know of two small Scotch deer being caught and sent to an English park, where they throve and soon grew as large as the rest of the herd—the comparatively mild winters and rich pasture soon told their tale. The greatest number of points that are authenticated on a red stag is sixty-six. On the frontispiece is a correct drawing of this head from a print of Riedinger's, and for which I am indebted to the kindness of my friend, Mr. R. R. Holmes, Her Majesty's Librarian at Windsor Castle. The head is still in existence, and was laid low by Frederich the First of Prussia, on the 18th September, 1696.

There can be little doubt, I imagine, that this very remarkable head must have been the result of some injury to the growing horn; but however that may be, there are the sixty-six points, and each one sufficient to hang a powder-flask on, which was the old stalking rule for claiming a point, and though powder-flasks have long been abolished at home, the rule still holds good.

The effect of a body hurt to a stag is generally very clearly to be seen in his horns: one that has been wounded and survived, or that has injured himself in any way, will rarely have a pair of good horns, and the one on the side nearest the damage will be small, malformed, almost pointless, or often there will be no horn at all.

As to the fencing of deer forests, if money be plentiful, it is undoubtedly a good plan to wire off the deer from the cultivated and low-lying lands adjoining. By so doing they are hindered from straying for miles in search of food and shelter in winter; the foresters are spared much hard and anxious work in endeavouring to drive them back and seeing that they are not poached; also, the farmers cannot grumble or claim compensation for damages done to their turnips. It is a mistake to surround a deer forest *entirely*. If it be done the fence is made so that at certain places deer can pass into the enclosed ground but cannot pass out, yet very few will ever pass in; and whenever a forest has been entirely surrounded by wire, in the course of a few years it has been found to be a mistaken and short-sighted policy. If it is done to a forest joining several others it is little short of folly, for all interchange of blood is prevented, and continually breeding in and in will surely tell a tale in the long run, and must deteriorate the deer both in quality and size. Apart from these considerations, stalking in an entirely fenced ground must reduce the sport very much to the level of shooting deer in a big park, for whatever blunders may be made, whatever way the wind blows it matters not; it may cost a shot, but the deer cannot get away; they are locked up, in a large space, but locked up all the same, and they are certain to be there the next day. "I'd as lief stalk a deer in a sheep-fank," an old stalker once said to me, on hearing of a neighbouring forest being totally enclosed, and his feeling on the matter I believe to be the correct and sportsmanlike one. For the benefit of the uninitiated, a "fank" is a large stone enclosure used by the shepherds to gather their sheep into.

In speaking of the weights of deer, as already mentioned, the writer intends his remarks to apply to "clean" weight. It has always seemed desirable that there should be throughout Scotland but *one* recognized system of weighing, and that this should be done without liver or heart. With these both left in the carcase

THE GRALLOCH.

it makes fully a stone extra weight, and hence the discrepancies one often hears of in adjoining forests, where the deer are always passing to and fro, and are identically the same, and yet in Mr. A's forest the deer will always be a stone heavier than in Mr. B's.

In forests where there are grouse shootings attached, and a salmon river also, it is by no means a difficult feat to bring off the "swagger" performance, as my young friends at Eton would call it, and kill flesh, fowl, and fish all in the same day. The first two—the stag and the grouse—are nearly certainties, and it is Mr. Salmon, with his capricious appetite, who usually stops the way to the achievement of the treble event.

As to the "gralloch," it is very rarely that the gentleman is called on to perform this necessary task for himself. Smoke your pipe, sit well to the leeward, and spy for other deer while it is in progress. Once only has it happened to me to be called on to perform this operation. The stalker had been sent home to fetch a pony to carry back a big stag I had shot, and which I was anxious to get home that night. During the man's absence of some five hours I found other stags, and successfully stalked and killed one; but pleased as I was with myself, the gralloch yet had much the same effect as a trip from Dover to Calais. I am not aware whether cattle, sheep, &c. have the same internal arrangements as the red deer, which has three distinct stomachs: the first, the bag into which the grass passes direct; a middle one, where it becomes more digested; and a third, which seems to be the fine and small grinding mill. This third stomach is of a very remarkable and wonderful construction, consisting of a number of tightly packed layers of membrane, resembling nothing so much in appearance and texture as the sage green plush gowns sometimes to be seen on æsthetic young ladies at the Grosvenor Gallery; stalkers call it the "monyplies," and if perfectly cleaned, a work of much trouble, they say it is excellent eating, but hitherto I have been content to take this statement on trust.

When cutting off the head of a stag that is considered worth setting up, insert the knife almost as low down as the join of the neck and the body; pass it round the skin, and then turn it back and sever the neck bone higher up. By doing this, the "Snowie" you may select to send it to for preservation will have an opportunity of setting up the head with a curve to the neck, which shows it off to much greater advantage. If you should happen to have a couple of niches, one on each side of a fire-place or side-board, this method of setting up is very desirable, as one head can be turned to the right and the other to the left, so that the two are looking towards each other, and thus they are far more ornamental to a room.

Spicer of Leamington, and Quartermain of Stratford-on-Avon are both first class at this description of work; but wherever the head be sent to for preservation, do not forget to state which way the head is to look.

As soon as the "last scene" is over, and a deer is cut up, the joints should be hung to dry; should there be no regular venison larder attached to the lodge, let them hang in some cool place where there is a good current of air, and no chance of rain being drifted on to them. Haunches should not be packed until they have hung a few days, and the fat has become well "set." A deal box is the best thing to pack them in—baskets are apt to let the flies pass in, and the rain also, whereas a good made box, well nailed down, does neither the one or the other. Stout canvas or matting is also used by some, and given fine weather it is as good as box or basket. Should, however, the haunch have to go many miles by mail-cart on a wet day, both this method of packing and the basket trick are certain to result in disappointment to the recipient: for meat that gets damp and wet, turns musty and mouldy by the time it arrives at the end of a thirty hours' journey, and then, if the cook be not very careful to pare off all the musty parts, before putting it to the fire, the whole joint will have a tainted, unpalatable, and perhaps downright unpleasant flavour. Whichever method of packing be chosen, the haunch should be nicely trimmed and floured, and if packed in canvas it should be wrapped in clean paper before sewing up.

The skull is cleaned by boiling for many hours; if a good large iron pot be used, several pairs of horns can be done at the same time, but great care must be taken that the brow antlers do not project over the sides of the pot and thus get charred: every year many good horns are spoilt in this manner; should such a misfortune happen, the horn may, perhaps, if not very badly burnt, be trimmed into shape, so as to make a point, and thus rendered presentable. A couple of flat files, one very rough, the other smooth, are the best implements for the purpose.

It is perfectly fair and legitimate to give the extreme points of the horns a slight scrape so as to render the tips white; a piece of glass is the best thing to use. This being done the horns look much better, and make a greater show when mounted on wooden shields and hung round the walls of a room. It is also absolutely true to nature, as any one can see for himself, if he will observe red deer after the stalking season is over, and in December and later, all the stags with good heads have the tips of their horns quite white and burnished—indeed, most October deer have this, but those killed early in September, especially in a late season, have not put on the finishing touches, which they accomplish by incessant and violent rubbing against the bunches of long rushes that grow so luxuriantly on the hills. The horns of deer killed with the velvet partly on, may be made a good colour by rubbing them with a handful of wet peat or by staining them with "Stevens' Oak Stain." A fine pointed pen should be used for writing the dates, &c., on the skull; a broad pointed one will cause the ink to run.

CHAPTER VI.

A DOUBLE EVENT—MY FIRST STAG—AND A MEMOIR OF LEGER DAY, 1875.

As a book on stalking might be considered incomplete without some description of various days on the hill, I have selected, as representative ones, four days from my game book which seemed to me extra exciting and varied. I do this with great diffidence, for I know there are so many who could do it better: and before further proceeding, I must ask the reader generously to bear in mind that this is a first attempt, and that my fingers are more accustomed to rifle, gun, and rod than to the pen.

I will start with the stalk that made the greatest impression on me, as it has ever done on others, and will ever do on many more, viz., my first stag. Nervously I hear the old hand exclaim, "Well! that *is* an ancient story; and what can be said about it that has not been said before?" Veteran, let me attempt to stir your pulses with the thoughts of days, for you, alas! gone by. Youthful novice, you will want no spur to incite you onwards to that red-letter day in your sport life, so let me try and tell how in one day I slew my first stag, and won a thousand pounds, thus bringing off a double event of unusually rare and pleasing nature.

On Monday, September the 13th, 1875, I awoke in St. James's Street, with the intention of going to Doncaster that afternoon to see the Leger run on the following Wednesday. With the hot water came my usual budget of morning letters: amongst them, one from a friend asking me to come up to him in the North; to excuse the short notice, and come as soon as possible. The letter concluded—"P.S. Mind you bring your rifle." Now this could only mean stags, and "keen" was no word to describe my longing to get a shot; for much as I had previously been in the North, I had never yet had the good fortune to be on ground where there were deer. I had, however, backed a horse for the Leger for an amount which for me was a plunge, and had made all arrangements to go and see him run for my money.

For a few minutes indecision got hold of me, and then the deer, and the name of the place I was going to, carried all before them, and hastening to my sitting-room, I sent off a wire to say I would start the same night. From that moment my bet was forgotten, and my whole thoughts concentrated on deer, and the fact that the day after to-morrow might bring me face to face with the chance I had been so long and so hotly wishing for.

In those days I did not possess a rifle, and was soon on my way to my old friend, Stephen Grant, to borrow the best he could lend me. He had only one left, in his shop—a ·500 bore just come back from The Cape to be overhauled. Gentlemen, he explained, were rather given to borrowing rifles, and did not buy them like guns, and with his usual anxiety to oblige his customers, he had lent all the second-hand rifles he had. This did not greatly surprise me, for out of the numbers that go North every year, there are but few who stalk regularly; and like myself, every guest asked to shoot where there are deer wants a rifle, and does not care to go to the expense of purchasing a new one for a few shots, and then perhaps for some seasons to come have no further opportunities. I took the only one I could get, and drove off with it, followed by many cautions to take a few sighting shots before going out. That same night saw me in the Limited Mail, a big cigar, a sound sleep, one whiskey and soda at Carlisle, more sleep, Perth, a wash and hearty breakfast, a change of trains, and a few hours later I was in mortal combat with a very tough chop in a Highland inn while the "machine" was being got ready. A lovely drive of twenty miles, and four o'clock that afternoon found me welcomed to a large and most comfortable house, by as kind a hostess as ever bid guest to cakes and ale. My host and his friends were still on the hill, and as I sat by the open window of the oak-panelled drawing-room, I could hear them popping away in the distance. Indeed, it was somewhat a strain on my politeness not to wish to be with them. Perhaps my hostess half divined the thought, for she soon suggested my trying the river before dinner, and furthermore, to inspire me, said that "Archie" (one of the keepers) had that morning reported it in good order, and plenty of fish up, although none had been caught yet, for it was the first autumn spate.

My acceptance of and thanks for the kind suggestion were more eloquent than lengthy. A rod was soon put together, and throwing a gaff over my shoulder, I was off to the river, which wanted no finding, for it ran at the foot of the lawn in front of the house. After a study of the water, and the selection of a fly that appeared about the right size, I strolled up stream in search of a pool; three likely-looking places were tried blank. I afterwards found out two of them were no good, and that the third only occasionally held a fish. Making my way higher up, I came to a very primitive wire suspension-bridge, and, "says I to myself, says I," if that is not a "catch" under it I never saw one. And right enough it was, and almost the first cast I was into a fish; a good deal of "give" for a few minutes, and plenty of "take" afterwards, and in a short time a goodly fourteen pounder laid on the bank.

Much pleased with my luck, and darkness coming on, I strolled back, and deposited my capture on the stone-slab near the front door, and put there for the purpose. The butler met me in the hall and showed me to my room, not without many a halt and longing look of admiration on my part, at the heads and horns that decorated every landing and passage. Descending to the drawing-room, I received a very hearty welcome, and many congratulations on my luck with the salmon —the first of the autumn season.

Dinner over — as the decanters commenced their round, the plans for to-morrow came on for discussion.

Two parties of two each were to go grousing, one could fish, and one could stalk. Thus, when my host asked, "Who will stalk?" my heart sank within me, for I expected to hear as noisy an "Ego" as when a school boy cries "Quis" to a slice of plum-cake. A short silence followed; and then one was so horribly tired, another had a violent attack of salmon-fishing, another had blistered his heel, and several preferred grousing. At length, catching my host's eye, it was settled I should go. Archie was warned for duty, and breakfast ordered for half-past five. From that moment until I was under way next morning I was in a state of anxious excitement. The smoking-room being reached, I was soon being cross-examined about my rifle—Who built it? what was the groving? how was it sighted? &c., &c., to all of which questions I could only say, "Don't know," and tell the story of how I procured one at all. So it was sent for, examined, and condemned, as one of the stops would not work after rough usage at The Cape.

My host sent for one of his, and put into my hand a splendidly finished ·450 express, saying, it was at my service. It was past midnight before we retired, and after setting the aneroid and cleaning a pair of binoculars, for, in addition to having no rifle, I also had no telescope, I turned into bed, thinking to myself this was fifty times better fun than Doncaster, and with a farewell sigh to the hundred and fifty pounds I had on next day's Leger, was soon sound asleep.

The next morning, having first assured myself it was fine, and the hills free of mist, I quickly dressed, breakfasted, and making sure nothing was left behind, found Archie at the door with two good-looking, rough and strong ponies. He was in high spirits at the wind blowing sharply from the best "airt," the east, and wished to go to the extreme end of the ground. Mounting my pony, I told him to give me a lead, and without a word more off he started at a trot. For about four miles we jogged along, the track being fairly good, and then we came to a hill, which Archie said was fifteen hundred feet high, and slowly we toiled up the zigzag path, at times approaching so near the edges of precipices, that if I had not seen his pony go first, and take no notice of them, I should have felt nervous about going so near. What with the steepness, the size and looseness of the stones, it was hard work for the ponies, and several times we had to stop and rest them; but at last the top was reached and the descent began over much the same ground, only the ponies went faster, and then another trot along a pretty level four miles more brought us to a small shepherd's bothy, where the ponies were to be left, and we had just been two hours doing the twelve miles.

We were soon off again, and after a scrambling walk of about two miles along the side of a loch, we reached the march. Then commenced the ascent of the overhanging hills, and in spite of the sharp east wind, I was something more than warm when we gained the first spying-place. Out came the glasses, Archie with his telescope, I with the binoculars. It was only a small corrie, and making sure nothing was there, I could not help turning my attention to the prospect around me. The day was perfect—a steady breeze, a bright blue sky, a few white clouds drifting rapidly overhead; the outlines of the very distant hills clear and well-defined—

a very ocean of them meet the eye; and of course to me the beauty of it all was more than doubled, for each hill was the haunt of the wild red deer. Was I not in the land of the stags? And did not Archie show me where to turn to look into the forests of Blackmount, Kinloch, Ben Alder, Dalness, Athol, and Glen Artney?

After spying this corrie we descended into it, and crossed to the top on the other side, seeing on our way very fresh tracks of deer, which rejoiced us much. On the summit of this fresh ridge of hills we had another spy, and again could find nothing; striking along the very top of this ridge to get to the next corrie, which Archie told me was the most likely one of all, we had a splendid walk on soft, mossy ground, as dry as a carpet; now and then starting a ptarmigan or a blue hare, and once stopping and getting out the glasses to watch the gyrations of two eagles circling about in the distance—altogether an enchanting and exhilarating tramp. At length we reached the end of the range, and stooping low as we crossed the sky-line, were soon comfortably seated, and spying the vast corrie that laid stretched at our feet. For fully half an hour we searched it up and down, and "dour" grew Archie's face when at last he shut up the glass with a snap of annoyance. Fully sharing his feelings, and finding it was one o'clock, I said we would eat our sandwich as soon as we could find spring water. Saying he thought we should get a spring a little way off, Archie volunteered to step down and see, if I would wait and come if he beckoned. Off he started, and to while away the time I again pulled out the glasses, and despairingly searched the ground afresh. Suddenly a thrill goes through me, and I can hardly keep the glass steady for excitement; another look, and there in that peat bog, what *is* that little red motionless speck? Can it be *him!* It is unlike anything my glass has found before, and frantically I beckon Archie back for the telescope. Quickly it was pulled out and brought to bear, and, hurrah! it is a "beast," at any rate. A small bit of the back was all that was visible, and it might yet turn out to be a hind.

After a few minutes of anxious suspense, the excitement increased as a grand pair of horns topped the hag, followed by the body of a fine stag. I can see him now as he shook the peat off him after his black bath, and then standing at attention for a few seconds, began to brouse.

Though at least a mile off, Archie told me in a whisper his plans for the stalk; while doing so our quarry again laid down, and we started to make a long *détour* to get into a burn beside which he was. This was done at best pace, and then began the stalk. While making this flank march, I explained to Archie that I was bent on doing the last three hundred yards quite alone. Revolt and astonishment came into his face, and he began to "argufy"; so to cut the matter short, I told him it *must* be that, or he could take the rifle and shoot him for himself. This settled the matter, and with a whispered, "Well, sir, you shall ha'e your wull," on we went again. Had I then known as much about it as I do now, I should never have thought of making the suggestion, for it was tantamount to risking my chance, and after it was all over Archie showed me the line I *ought* to have taken, and which would have brought me much nearer to my quarry, had I allowed him to take me up; but in my ignorance and excitement I had made up my mind to have as much of the honour and glory as possible. A very steep clamber now brought us to the spot where the burn came tumbling out of the corrie. Suddenly Archie sank quietly flat, and the look he gave me as he muttered, "Shape! the beggars!" would at any other time have sent me into fits of laughter. However, there they were, some dozen of them, right in our line of advance, and half startled; once wholly so, our chance would be spoilt. There was nothing for it but to wait, and after half an hour of anxiety they at length fed away quietly. Almost crawling, and moving very cautiously for fear of meeting more sheep, we entered the burn, which had cut a deep channel through the peat, and gave us splendid shelter, if somewhat wet and dirty. About an hour and a half since, lying by the side of this burn, we had left our stag, and here I parted with Archie, with many injunctions to "mind the shape," and "tak' plenty o' time." After crawling on hands and knees some distance, I took a peep a-head through a bunch of old heather. To my great joy he was still there, some four hundred yards distant, but he was up and feeding. Crawling on as fast as I could, another look showed me I was only about two hundred and fifty yards off. He was feeding away from the burn, striding from patch to patch of grass, taking a bite here, a bite there, and tossing his head to the wind every few seconds, standing at times as if petrified, and staring hard, which made me very uncomfortable; and yet it was impossible to help admiring the grace and freedom of his every movement. As he turned away I wormed myself like a snake out of the burn into a patch of heather leading up to him; and now I seemed almost to pull myself along by my eyelids. Each time he raised his head I was flat and motionless, each time he resumed his feeding I wormed myself slowly nearer, till at last I could no further go, the thick heather being burnt. It seemed a very long shot, and he was standing head on to me. However, I saw at a glance it was now or never; so I put up the sight, resolved if he moved away from me to fire, and if he came nearer to wait. It was soon settled. He strode away, and then for one instant stood broadside to me as if carved in marble. Whether something had alarmed him will never be known, for, taking a quick aim, I pressed the trigger with a beating heart. Springing to my feet to clear the smoke and use the second barrel, there was nothing in sight! Wildly I looked about, despairingly I sighed, "Missed, by all that's riling!" Then came yells from Archie, "Run up! run up! well done you!" and I dashed towards the place where the stag had stood, and on the other side of a knoll *there he laid*—not dead, as a vicious sweep of the horns warned me. Archie was soon up, and going in behind him, seized his horns, while I administered the *coup de grâce* in front—both operations requiring some little coolness. He was a good fat stag of ten points, and weighed seventeen stone clean the next day. As it was my first, Archie was all for smearing my face over with blood for luck; but I compromised, and escaped with a large cross on the back of each hand.

Stepping back to the place I fired from, I made it just one hundred and seventy-five paces; and then while Archie was performing the gralloch, I started off across the corrie to where we had left our luncheon; and as it was now near four o'clock, right glad I was to get it. When we had refreshed, and talked it over, and had a pipe, it was time to start home; so propping the stag open with a large long stone to allow him to cool quickly, and fastening a bunch of paper to his horns to flutter in the breeze and scare away the ravens, with a parting look at our quarry we started on the return journey. Home was reached a little before nine o'clock, as our progress in the dark was very slow. I now began to see why no one else had volunteered for the day's sport. To get up at five o'clock, ride twenty-four miles, and stalk all day on ground lying mostly at an angle of forty-five degrees, would be quite enough for most of us three days a-week. A hot tub, a good dinner, and I was soon feeling fresh again. My host came and smoked a cigar with me while I ate and told him of my adventures, and how delighted I had been with my day.

We were chatting merrily away when the door opened, and almost unnoticed I found the butler standing by my side with a small silver waiter.

"Telegram for you, sir; the cart was down for supplies to-day, and brought this from the station, sir." The Leger, and the fact that it was run that day, had been till that moment clean forgotten. Tearing it open —again hurrah! hurrah! Craigmillar first—and had not one of the safest and most courteous of book-makers laid me a thousand to one hundred and fifty against him! This was indeed a red-letter day—my first stag had "come off!" my plunge had come off! Reader, what more can I say?—good spirits are catching, and long and loud the laughter rose in the smoking-room that night.

CHAPTER VII.

FINE WEATHER STALK, WITH WIND AND LIGHT AND LUCK ALL IN OUR FAVOUR, AND HOW SEPTEMBER 3RD, 1881, I KILLED MY FIRST "ROYAL," GETTING HIM HOME THAT SAME EVENING.

THE scene of this day's adventures opens in a plain-built Highland lodge; going to the east it was over thirty miles to the railway-station, and ten to the nearest baker's or farmer's; going north, south, or west there was no habitation nearer than double that distance. A long, low white house, with slate roof; stoutly built was it; solid it had need to be, for it is the highest inhabited house in Scotland, and lies just seventeen hundred and forty feet above sea-level. There, with double force and power the wind can blow, the rain can fall, the snow can beat and drift, and the ice-king plant his iron grasp.

No carriage, dog-cart, or "machine" had ever driven up to the door, for eight miles off the road came to an end. On the occasion of my first advent, as I watched the "machine" depart, leaving me standing on the heather, surrounded by gun and rifle-cases, portmanteaus, cartridge-boxes and wraps, I began to speculate how all this was ever to get to its destination. My reverie is broken by the appearance from behind a stone dyke of a couple of sturdy gillies, one of them leading a strong pony with a saddle on, the other at the head of another pony harnessed to a very small two-wheel cart. They salute, and one of them hands me a note from his master. It is simply to say, "Come on as fast as you can; my mare, Maggie, knows the way, so if it gets dark throw the reins on her neck, and she will bring you safely, and you will be here long before the luggage-cart." As it happens, this particular day the sun is setting in a mass of orange-sky. As I face to my destination in the west, the hills in their deep shadows look black, cold, and distant; the air is chilly, and I feel stiff after the twenty-six mile drive and the long journey from London. A short way a-head the pony track seems to disappear, and altogether an "uncanny" feeling comes over me. However, Maggie is mounted, and off she goes at a pleasant trot, and men and cart and luggage are quickly lost to view. Soon the trot becomes a walk; there are rocks, big stones, bogs and holes, but Maggie steers clear of them all, and directly the going is once more good, she breaks into a trot again of her own accord, till by the time a couple of miles are covered I place implicit faith in her good sense, and abandon all to her guidance. And so one jogs along, up hill and down hill, and the hoofs of the pony fall silently on the soft track. On either hand a dark sea of heather, overhead the stars were just beginning to show, and facing me rises the jagged outline of an amphitheatre of black hills against the deep crimson sky, still lit with the glow of the setting sun. In about an hour I begin to wonder if Maggie *can* have gone the wrong way, and feel half inclined to stop and wait for the cart. At last I do so, and listen for it, but in vain. The mare shakes her head impatiently, and on she jogs again, carrying me safely through a roaring burn. Another half-hour passes, I strike a light and look at the watch, and begin to feel *sure* I have lost the way; then another half-hour goes by, and just as I am quite certain of being a waif and a stray, a sudden shine of lights and smell of peat-smoke puts a pleasant end to all uncertainties, and in a few minutes more the journey is ended. I have ridden and walked that track many a time since, but these were my sensations then, and I never yet knew any one do it the first time, but what he had a good deal to say about it over his dinner. In the teeth of a gale from the west, and the rain driving into one's face, it was indeed something to talk about. It will be seen from this that we are, as the guide books say, in a "remote and inaccessible" part of Scotland.

On this 3rd of September, 1881, three of us have just finished breakfast, and are standing round the peat and wood fire preparatory to starting for a day's grousing. The room has four windows in it, one looking north, two looking east, and another facing south—a splendid view of moor and loch and mountain to be seen from each. Strange to say, the drawing-room, the library, the smoking-room, and gun-room all had the same view and the same arrangement of windows; but this was accounted for by the room we were in serving the purposes of all, and dining-room to boot. It was a bright sunny morning, with a gentle breeze driving large white fleecy clouds across the sky, and the moving shadows

G

rolling up the mountains and across the moor made a perfect picture of a wild landscape.

Lazily I went to the window looking south to see more of the view, and as I threw it open to get a better look-out, the shadows rolled off stag-famed Ben y Vricht, and a flood of most brilliant sunshine illumined its face; from the very summit of the rocky and precipitous crest right down to the more gentle slopes of the heather-clad base. So very sharp and clear did it seem to stand out, that although four miles away, I turned to the mantelpiece to reach down a spy-glass, remarking, "It is so very bright that, in spite of the distance, one might see deer if they were there." "No," said my host, "it is too far, except by any chance there were a hundred of them together, and they were moving." However, kneeling down, and resting the glass on the window-sill, it was brought to a focus, and lo and behold! there actually, as if by magic, were quite a hundred deer, trotting in a mass across a bright green strip of grass. The discovery is proclaimed with great excitement, and in no time every spy-glass on the premises was turned on the herd. My host looked at me; I looked at him; and our thoughts showed themselves in the eyes of both. "Who shall go?" was the question that propounded itself unconsciously to each of us. The matter was soon settled, for my friend, with rare self-denial, and ever anxious to show sport to his friends, said to me, "Well, as you found them, you shall go after them; with this wind you *must* go round, so I will post myself in a pass to which they may come." This resolved, our third gun, who luckily did not much care for stalking, went off to his grouse beat. By ten o'clock I also was away with Donald McCallum; we started as if we were going to walk right from the herd, but after about three miles in that direction we began to turn their flank, and by twelve o'clock found ourselves about a mile from them; the greater part were lying down in a large half circle, the hinds at either end, and all the stags in the centre. Even at that distance our glasses easily showed us there were many very fine heads amongst them; one especially in every way seemed to tower above all his fellows. From the position they were then in it was impossible to approach nearer till they moved, for there was a large flat between us and them, and the hill they were resting on commanded every inch of it. We pushed on, however, to the edge of this flat, which brought us to within about half a mile; here we had to halt, and creeping to a heathery knoll, we pulled out the glasses and examined them one by one at our leisure. Soon we made out that the stag we had already noticed as being bigger than all the rest was a most undoubted "royal." I at once impressed on Donald that *that* was the deer I *must* shoot at. Never yet had I had a chance at such a one, and have him I must, so would shoot at no other, and intended chancing a shot at him at three hundred yards in preference to firing at another one at eighty, however good he might be. We counted more than forty stags, and judged there were double as many hinds—truly a splendid sight. In about an hour the hinds began to rise and feed, and in a short time all but two small "staggies" followed their example, and fed away from us over the hill top and out of sight. The question now was, could we venture to creep across the flat without being detected by these two little "beasties"? We determined to try; and then began one of the longest, most tedious, and wettest of creeps I have ever had to undertake. The flat was simply a morass, and no hillock or water-course to shelter us higher than two feet or deeper than one. Forth we crept, as if we had been own brothers to the original serpent; in a moment we are wet from breast to knees, sinking well over our elbows at every movement, often having to wait motionless for many minutes while these two little despicable and provoking stags ceased feeding and gazed about them. When we were three parts across, to our great joy they turned off after the herd, and pleasant indeed was the relief of standing up and beginning a run; but we had not done with them yet, for one turned back; luckily we saw his horns coming into sight, and down we dropped as flat and still as two stones. This quite did away with any pretence of being dry, for in going down I slipped, and fell on my back in a pool, and there laid for some time, afraid to stir hand or foot; the cause of our trouble, having unconsciously put us to all the annoyance possible, at length turned and went off, and in safety we got to the hillock at the edge of the flat. Here we took the rifle out of the case, and began to crawl up; having advanced about a hundred yards in this way, the hinds could be seen on either side of us, and almost within shot; and as they were feeding quietly and no stags were visible, it became next door to a certainty that they were all on the other side of a small hill some sixty feet high, and not very far in front of us. Again it is a debated question of crossing the intervening space; the ground, however, favoured us, and slipping into a burn, we arrived at the foot of the hill, on the other side of which we expected the stags to be. I now took the rifle, and pulling back the stops, crept gently up, with Donald at my elbow. We were within ten feet of the top, and brimful of hope, when an old cock grouse flew off the very summit, crowing as if his life depended on the noise he made. "Quick, sir! run up!" whispers Donald, and together we dash forward, and crouch behind a big stone at the top, but only to see the whole herd heading direct for my host's hiding-place, which was about a mile away.

It is annoying beyond everything to be beaten like this just at the very last minute; there are several good stags trotting off and offering fair shots at about one hundred and twenty yards, but my prize—my royal—is so covered by others I could get no possible chance at him. "Take that one; you'll get no other," says Donald, as he points out a good shootable beast, but I was so angry that I would not, and sat watching them all go right away with the rifle on the royal, and resolved to take any chance at him, however poor. At last his head and neck is clear, and crack! crack! both bullets are sent after him, much as if shooting at a grouse, but with no other effect than to put the whole herd into a violent gallop. It was an almost impossible shot, and though knowing it, a feeling of utter disgust took possession of me. I mechanically reloaded, not with any intention of shooting again, but from pure force of habit. An old hind was leading the herd, and suddenly, for no reason that could be made out, she turned sharp to the left, taking the whole lot with her, and they began to gallop past us broadside on, about two hundred yards away. We instantly recognized the altered position of affairs. Again hope runs high as Donald whispers, "Steady, sir; that's him, last but three." I bring the foresight about two feet in front of his chest, and press the trigger; the royal falls stone dead in his tracks, without so much as a struggle. Overjoyed at this, the other barrel was emptied at the best stag to be seen clear of the rest, and he also fell mortally wounded. We rushed in at once, but the royal needed no attention, and I stayed to admire him while Donald gave the *coup de grâce* to the other one. The big stag was struck right in the very centre of the heart, and though of course it was where the bullet was intended to go, I could not help feeling it was very lucky to have placed it so exactly; for he was going as hard as he could gallop, and we paced it two hundred and twelve paces: and allowing for small undulations it might fairly be put at one hundred and eighty yards as the crow flies. I fully intended to put the rifle sight rather more in front of the smaller stag, but he was hit a foot behind the heart, through the kidneys, and fell two hundred and forty paces distant. By the time they were gralloched, lunch eaten, and the stalk discussed, it was near three o'clock. Suddenly it struck me that it was Saturday, and unless we could get the royal home that evening,

MY FIRST ROYAL

he would have to lay out where he fell till Monday—a period of nearly forty-eight hours, and foxes, eagles, or very heavy rain might all combine to spoil him. This was not to be thought of. The lodge was but four miles in a bee line, so telling Donald to look sharp and go back for a pony as fast as he could, I volunteered to wait his return and help him to put the stag on the saddle, for no one man could have done this. Off went Donald; and seating myself by my prize I lit a pipe, and had ample time to admire anew his goodly proportions and noble antlers—a perfectly shaped "chandelier" horn, of great substance and width, with very long, strong brow antlers, as were also the three points on each top. Since then I have carefully looked at many royal heads hanging round the walls of friends' houses, and have noticed but few that can "take the shine" out of the one that then laid by my side, which I will confess had already become an object of speculation as to whether it would be given me to grace the walls of my very small dining-room.

Time passed on, and also began to pass very slowly, when two shots in the distance called me to attention; putting the spy-glass on to the place from whence the sound came, I found my host and his man working a brace of dogs. From his pass he had seen that the deer were away, and sending back for his gun, he was having an afternoon with the grouse, and shooting towards me. I quickly joined him, and he shot up to where my trophies lay, getting eight brace on the way; arrived there, we sat down and waited for Donald's re-appearance. At last about six o'clock he came; we soon had the pony loaded, and thought to save our daylight and be home in good time. The Fates, however, willed otherwise: ere a quarter of a mile had been negotiated the girths of the deer-saddle broke, and stag and saddle came tumbling off; it did not seem a bad break, was quickly mended, and the advance resumed. A short distance more was covered when the girths again gave way, and deer and saddle rolled together into a deep pool of a burn and disappeared entirely, save the two hind legs. With a deal of pulling from all four of us they were hauled out, and we once more set to work to repair damages; it took longer than the first operation, but satisfied at length that our work would now hold, the pony was saddled and the royal replaced. Again we proceed in comfort for some distance, when a sudden effort of the pony to keep his feet in a stumble undid all, and saddle and stag laid at our feet for the third time. Both the gillies were now all for leaving him, but we determined not to be beaten without one more try, so to work again we went. It was now nearly dark, but by the aid of a box of wax matches, and with the assistance of the united boot-laces of the whole party, we again made matters good for another start. This had taken the best part of an hour to do, and it was now quite dark; but by holding up the stag at every rough place, we at length reached home a few minutes before ten o'clock. We found our grouse shooter, who had brought home twenty-seven brace, well-nigh famished, as he had politely waited dinner for us, and in ten minutes we were all at table, discussing the events of the day. Later on my host sent me to bed in a most happy frame of mind, by telling me to have the head packed and sent off to be set up for myself. The next day, though it was "the Saabeth," we weighed him, twenty-one stone clean, without heart or liver. Since then I have killed plenty of deer each season, but that still remains my first and only shot at a "royal." As each year comes round I live in hopes of securing a head worthy to hang opposite to this one—the subject of a very red-letter day in my sport life. The stalk described was remarkable from the fact of our having got up to such a large herd of deer at the very first attempt; and also, it was noticeable from our getting a fairly easy *broadside* shot after we had fired two barrels at them. As illustrating the great difficulty of getting up to a large herd of deer, I give an extract from my game book.

"1883, Sept. 28—Found a very good stag in the flat. I was after him from ten o'clock till dusk He had eighty hinds with him, and after seven distinct stalks we were eventually defeated. I did not get a shot all day."

CHAPTER VIII.

A DAY WITH EVERYTHING AGAINST US—BAD WEATHER —BAD LUCK—AND BAD SHOOTING.

ON the 5th October, 1884, I started on foot from the same lodge in high latitudes. It was a dull, dark morning; the tops of the highest hills had not discarded their night-caps, and there was hardly any wind to induce them to lay them aside. It is a long steep pull up to the top of the hill above the lodge; master and man were both very hot before we were at the watershed. Arrived there, we found ourselves in the mist, but pushed boldly on in hopes of finding Corrie Craegacht clear, only to be disappointed, for it grew thicker and thicker, till we could not see twenty yards in front of us. To go on would have been spoiling our ground, so we sat down and waited, talking in whispers, for it was a noted corrie for deer, and they might even be close at hand. In the course of an hour we were both shivering with cold, and began to discuss turning back and shooting grouse in the valley. Then there came a puff of wind, boring a hole in the mist, and disclosing two stags and five hinds feeding on a grassy flat in the crown of the corrie about five hundred yards beneath us; then the wind died away, and the mist came rolling on thicker than ever. No question now, however, of going back; there we would wait all day, if needs be, and we sit straining our eyes and trying to see. Fifty yards off a ptarmigan is croaking; we are glad to know his whereabouts, so that he may have a wide berth whenever the time does come to make a start, which we postponed until we could get another peep at our quarry, so as to be quite sure of their position; in the thickest mist deer can always see their pursuers long before they themselves are visible to the weaker optics of poor mortals. At last the wind freshens, the mist parts in fantastic shapes, and we see our quarry feeding up a burn with all their heads well down into it; flat on our backs, and watching them closely, we begin to punt ourselves down-hill by our elbows. A hind's head is raised; we are as immovable as the rocks around us; feeding is resumed, and on we push; then down comes the mist, and we take advantage of it to advance on foot, but keeping very low, till we judge we shall be within a long shot the next time we can see. A third time the mist lifts, but only to show us the deer had moved up-hill, about a quarter of a mile. It keeps fair, and we crawl steadily upwards; they are still feeding up the burn, and only the tops of their backs just visible; little brown specks, which, near as they are, the unpractised eye might easily fail to discover. We are soon about a hundred yards from them; five paces in front is a big rock behind which we can hide in comfort and wait for a fair chance; we are close to it, when a hind's head pops up out of the burn, and in a second we are detected. Giving a loud bark of alarm, off she goes up-hill, the rest following; last of all are the two stags, offering a fair three-quarter side shot. They are going at a fast "slinging" trot, and although rather difficult shots, they should certainly be killed, one at any rate, if not both; but my two barrels are emptied in vain! "You were over him each time, sir; but the mist is going, and maybe we will get a better chance presently." So says Donald. And thinking a great deal, but saying little, I merely reply, "Then go ahead, and let me see if I can do better."

The corrie being a very large one, we sat down and spied the opposite face and tops; finding nothing, we crossed it in a good hour's hard climbing, which was well rewarded by finding a solitary stag in a very small corrie. As Donald shuts up his glass with a snap, his face brightens as he murmurs,—"If he stays where he is, sir, you will get a very fine chance." A retrograde movement is executed, and then after a study of the wind and the ground, we find we can walk almost right up to him. Off we go at best pace for a short mile, and our quarry should be just over the top of the small hill we are about to ascend; we mount it quietly, so as not to be out of breath when we come to the summit. Only some seventy yards remain to be climbed, when, to our dismay, a single sheep sprang out of a hole almost at our feet, and galloped off as fast as he could in front of us. As soon as he has topped the sky-line we race after him; to have started before would only have frightened him more and made him run faster; but we reach the top only to find the sheep standing where the stag had been, and he himself quietly trotting away some four hundred yards distant. This was very hard lines, as the ground was cleared of sheep, and this one must have strayed a long distance from his companions—at the moment it almost seemed as if on purpose to get in our way. Having blessed that sheep, eaten our sandwich, and discussed what was best to be done, a gleam of sunshine coming through the clouds, we settled not to follow this stag, but to go on to the end of the ground, and see what that would do to change the luck.

Another climb, another spy, this time blank, there remained but one more corrie in front of us. It is getting late, and we push on as fast as we can to the next top. There is no need to spy the corrie, for on one side of it are quite two hundred deer of all sorts, and easily visible to the naked eye. Between us and them the ground is so bare that it is impossible to approach. To try from below, for the same reason, is equally out of the question; to venture it from above would be certain to give them our wind. In another hour it will be dark, so if anything is to be done it must be attempted quickly. There is only one thing for it: I am to go off alone, and post myself in a pass below, while Donald goes round above them and gives them his wind. There will be a good chance of their coming to me when disturbed. Off I dash down-hill, and in twenty minutes am safely in my place, about six hundred yards from the herd. Anxiously I watched them. Suddenly there is a move, and every head stops feeding and goes up; all stand at attention, and turned to the hill top over which Donald is coming. Thus for a few seconds they stand as if petrified, and then they are all heading towards me at a trot. They come on for about two hundred yards, and then stop and look back ; but this does not trouble me, for I am in the pass, and they have nowhere else to go to. I pick up the glass, and notice the whereabouts in the herd of a few very good stags, and casting it up to the sky-line beyond, see Donald coming into view; then they all begin to walk quietly towards my hiding-place, looking back continually. The leading hinds are not three hundred yards away; the stops are drawn back, the rifle full cock, when, horror of horrors! I feel a distinct puff of wind *at my back*! A few seconds after they all come to a dead stop, and look suspiciously in my direction; see me I know they cannot. But again comes that dreadful breeze, only this time stronger and longer; suddenly the hinds bark, and the whole herd is galloping off at right angles, and it is too dark to shoot with any certainty at that distance. Alas! the wind had changed and betrayed me.

Now, I make it a rule to allow these catastrophes to cause as little annoyance as possible, and take them as philosophically as most, always provided they do not arise from any bungling on my own part. So I sat down and lit a pipe, pulled out the cartridges, and waited in the dusk for Donald to join me. It had now clouded over ominously, and large drops were splashing down. With an ugly sound the wind began to sigh in nasty gusts through the corrie, and by the time we had joined forces again it was nearly dark, raining in torrents, and the wind increasing in force every minute. We had four miles to go to reach the track, and then another five to the Lodge. As we stumbled and floundered over the moor, it soon became pitch dark; it thundered, lightened, hailed, snowed, and rained by turns, and Dame Nature did her best to turn out superior samples of each for our benefit.

Just before reaching the track Donald lost his shoe in a peat bog, and though he lit all the matches we both had (a Highlander and a sailor can always light a match in a gale, and both *face* the wind to do it), we could not find the shoe, and it was not until next day that he retrieved it. Now, considering it was a pitch dark night, and we were on the moor, it seemed to me an extraordinary clever feat to be able to go straight back to the spot; but Donald did it, and when questioned only said, "Well, sir, I just ken the ground."

We arrived home about half-past nine, rather tired and very wet. As our rule was never to wait for each other after half-past eight, I found my host finishing his dinner. If I had been unlucky, he had made ample amends to the goddess of the larder: using only five cartridges he had bagged three good stags, and two blue hares on the way home, near the Lodge, and where the shots could disturb no deer. My own misadventures are soon forgotten in discussing his success, and hoping to imitate it next day. Thus ended one of those unlucky twelve hours which are often the lot of the deer-stalker, but without which it would not be half the sport it is. To go out day after day, never to miss, never to be disappointed, never to have any difficulties to vanquish or hardships to face, would speedily do away with the science, sport, and fun of the pursuit. It is almost the one British sport left in which but little favouritism can be shown. All that can be done in that way is to give the favoured guest the likeliest beat to stalk on: after that the deer treat all as equals. Any one, no matter his rank or calling, if he wants to outwit them, must run, crawl, creep, lie still, face heat and cold, wind and rain, must toil up-hill and stumble down-hill, and slide or climb—all and each exactly as the *deer dictate*. It is this that makes the sport so highly prized, and in spite of **Mr. Bryce**, *et hoc genus omne,* long may it flourish.

CHAPTER IX.

STALKING EN LUXE—A LONG DAY IN A LARGE FOREST
WITH VARYING LUCK.

WE will now change the venue from Perthshire to Forfarshire—a county equally as wild and beautiful, though differing in the character of the mountains, which are rounder and "lumpier." This in some respects makes the stalking more difficult, for the ground not being so rough and broken, the shots have to be taken at longer distances.

Here also we are a long drive from the railway-station —twenty-three miles, but with the difference that there is a good carriage-road to the hall-door. The house also is large and luxurious, and surrounded by nicely wooded grounds, lying nine hundred feet above the sea, and altogether as picturesquely placed and comfortable a dwelling as one could wish for.

On the 17th September, 1885, a splendid autumn morning had somewhat hurried us through breakfast, and my host, with his big cigar well alight, and I, are quickly in the saddle, and trotting along the side of Loch Lee to overtake the foresters, who have gone on in advance. In pleasant converse we ride along side by side for about two miles, then the track narrows and forces us into single file. Soon we overtake the foresters, each followed by a gillie, and they in turn followed by two ponies with deer-saddles, led by their respective men. The hills now begin to close in on us, and as the procession winds along in single file, the four ponies, their two riders, and six attendants make quite a show.

We follow the course of a mountain stream for another three miles, seeing several large herds of hinds on our way. They do not appear to mind us much, merely moving quietly off to the hill tops, and there staying to watch us out of sight. As long as we go on they are content; if we stop and look they bolt at once.

Arrived at the place at which we are to part, we dismount, and wish each other good luck. My host, with his invariable kind courtesy, has given me the best beat and the head forester; he and his attendants strike away to the right, while I with mine go to the left. Before doing so the pony-man is instructed where to look out for us towards evening, so that I may get a ride home. Then the business of the day commences. Ascending the hill facing us we sit down for our first spy, and quickly see a lot of hinds right in front of us; to the left of these are others, with one good stag amongst them; and then to the left of these again another herd of hinds, so that our quarry is in the centre of the two. Now, what are we to do? To try and crawl direct to the stag would certainly expose us to the view of one of the other herds. The direction of the wind forbids all idea of getting round them; we feel half disposed to leave them alone; but then if we are to go forward at all we *must* disturb them.

It is decided it is better to have a try at a very difficult and daring stalk. The deer in front of us are lying at the top of a hill with a rocky face, falling sheer some sixty feet; but John Mitchell knows well enough, that if we can only reach it there is room to crawl along on the rocky ledges running parallel to the top. Signing to the gillie to stay where he is with the dog, we creep as flat as we can to the spur of the hill, and then descend to the edge of a precipice some three hundred feet deep; having gained this shelter, we can pick our way uphill amongst the rocks, taking great care not to slip. We do so till we are level with the hinds below which we want to pass; turning sharp to the left, then begins a very hard crawl to the knees, for it is over rocks. We push our way along this ledge, holding on by old heather roots and tufts of grass growing in the fissures of the rock, till we are right under the whole herd of hinds, and *not thirty yards* from them! Shall we get past without being detected? Noiselessly and with extreme caution we progress till we come into full view of the third lot, which doubles our difficulties. They are well below us, however, and deer are not much given to looking up-hill; although in a case of this sort they are more liable than usual to do so, as they like occasionally to see what the others are about. Thus very gently we creep on: in another fifty yards we can ascend the face and be within shot of the herd where the stag is. Forty yards are safely traversed, when one of us dislodges a large piece of loose rock, and down it falls with a clatter and great thud as it reaches the heather. I take the rifle from John, and we quicken our crawl. With my left hand I pull myself to a hillock, off which I mean to shoot, but on raising my head gently, find the whole herd alarmed, and standing in a thick cluster, and the stag is head on to me. My eyes are full of dust and perspiration; as I push the rifle forward there is clearly not a second to be lost. Suddenly they wheel; the stag comes broadside to me and pauses; another moment, and it seems certain they will all be off, so I, like a duffer, hurry my aim and miss handsomely, and so quickly do they turn and crowd together that there is no time to fire the second barrel. Annoying enough after all the toil we had taken, as it only wanted a kill to make this the most brilliant and exciting bit of stalking I had ever seen. Complimenting John on his part of the business, and doing very much the reverse to my share, we took a cup of water and started off again. After tramping some distance, we found five stags and a few hinds in a small corrie. Making a short and easy stalk, we were soon within range, and a nice nine-pointer bit the dust to the first barrel, the only shootable stag amongst the lot.

I took my lunch while the gralloch went on, and that finished we were on the tramp again, quickly finding a lot of very heavy stags. We commenced to stalk them on a side wind, and whether we sailed too near to the wind, or whether a grouse we put up disturbed them this deponent sayeth not. It was probably the latter, but off they all galloped along the side of a very big round hill. Directly they were out of sight John jumped up and went off full tilt, saying he felt sure of meeting them on the other side. I ran after him till I could run no longer, but on he went, always beckoning me to follow; so again I raised a trot and stumbled along after him—wet through with perspiration, and my heart bumping against my ribs as if it would knock its way out. Again I stop to a walk, again I am beckoned on, this time *frantically;* and once more I raise a trot, and then, thank goodness, I find I am going on the flat, and soon, better still, stumbling along down-hill. There are a few big rocks in front of us, and to my great relief, behind one of these John drops. He pulls the stops back and hands me the rifle, whispering, "They are no by yet." A few minutes pass, and I am not puffing and blowing quite so hard as I hear him say, "They are coming now." And so they do—a splendid sight to see. I whisper to him to pick me out a big one; some twenty pass us and he makes no sign, then he murmurs, "Now take this one just coming into sight." I sit firm, and planting my elbows on my thighs, press the rifle to my shoulder. As I do so comes the caution: "Aim low, they are barely fifty yards," and just in time to remind me; so lowering the sight till I could almost see daylight under my quarry, I press the trigger, and the gallant stag drops almost motionless in his tracks. So quickly do the others turn and break down-hill that there is no chance offered of using the other barrel. I am, however, quite satisfied; and while the gillie does the gralloch, I lay flat on my back, and with eyes shut soon recover my breath. Here follows a pipe and a drop of whiskey, and over it I thank John warmly for his friendly caution of "aim low," for when he whispered I had the fore-sight right in the centre of the deer's heart, just as I should have held at a *hundred yards*, and had I pulled the trigger then the bullet would assuredly have gone over my victim's back; so I had to thank my cool and active friend for a kill, as well as a very pretty run in. Only a most extraordinary knowledge of the ground and the pace of the deer could have enabled him to time it as he did.

These three stalks, two of which had been most exciting, and affording a brilliant display of the science as carried on by a past master in the art, had only whetted my appetite for more. It was but four o'clock, and this bright day we could see to shoot till nearly six, and it wanted no persuasion on my part to induce John to give me another chance. Leaving the dog and the gillie, we were soon a couple of miles away from our last kill, and on the highest ground in the forest; we were close to the Glen Muick march, and beyond that we could see into the forests of Balmoral, Mar, and Ben Avon—a glorious scene of hills and peaks and valleys. We sat down to spy, and found a herd of some twenty stags feeding near the march on a very large flat: some of them were lying, the rest standing up, but not moving about, so as time was short the only chance of a shot was a creep across this flat. This was a very difficult matter, but by dint of taking advantage of every depression, and keeping ourselves quite flat, till I felt as if the curse of the serpent was on me, we got to about three hundred yards from them. Here we laid, hoping a stag or two would feed nearer to us. After a time,

A VERY LONG SHOT.

those which had been lying got up and joined the rest, and all fed gently away from us.

"It is a very long shot, sir; but try it, for you will get no other chance," says John. I shake my head and decline, but am again encouraged to risk it; so pushing the rifle quietly over a tussock of grass, I pick out a good stag standing motionless and broadside on. I take a long and careful aim, and press the trigger, and to my surprise almost, the stag rolls over; but, alas! only to regain his feet and dash off after his flying comrades.

We keep perfectly still, and our glasses show that the fore leg is broken close to the shoulder. We watch them out of sight, and as they disappear over the sky-line we rise. John says to me, "Yon's a very good beast, and it will be a pity to lose him; but if we follow it will make us very late home." I tell him not to mind; so off we start on their tracks. Arrived where we lost sight of them, we sit down and spy, but there is not a sign; proceeding again, we come to a burn, and John opines we should find the stag lying by the side of this. Cautiously and slowly we advance, keeping a sharp look-out, for the banks are steep and broken, and we may walk right on to him if he be there. Presently John stops short, and gently reduces his six foot four by a foot or more. He hands me the rifle with a grin on his face and a satisfied twinkle in his sharp eyes, and bending to my ear whispers, "I can see the tops of his horns close to us," he points to a little hill and waves me up. I crawl in, and soon see the wounded deer. Poor fellow! he is lying down, but looking about on all sides, and very miserable. A few seconds elapse, and as the report of the rifle rings through the hills his troubles are over, and he lies prone upon the peat. It is a fine fat stag of nine points. John did the needful as quickly as possible, for it was already getting dusk; and taking a small nip of whiskey each, we start off best pace to reach the ponies, which are quite ten miles away. Luckily it is not very dark, and we get along well side by side, grievously scaring sundry ptarmigan; and as John is a pleasant and well-informed companion, and can talk on most subjects, we are speedily chatting in strong language about Mr. Bryce's Access to Mountains Bill, and speculating whether the Rads will ever pass it.

Then comes a break-neck descent, and we find ourselves at John's cottage, and at the gate stands my pony ready saddled. Wishing him a hearty good night, and highly delighted with a splendid day's sport, I trot off along the loch side, and a quarter to ten sees me tubbed and dressed in the dining-room. The ladies have left, and cigars are going, while I eat my dinner and hear my host's adventures. He also has done well, getting two stalks, and killing a good stag each time, he was comfortably home by half-past seven.

Our third rifle, who had started before us in the morning, in a totally different direction, now joined in and told me his adventures: he also had had two shots and bagged one nice stag, and in addition had met with a very curious incident. After he had killed his stag, the forester with him had asked, as a favour, that he would go about a quarter of a mile out of his way to enable him to visit a fox-trap he had set some ten days before. It was baited with part of the gralloch

A GOLDEN EAGLE TRAPPED.

of a deer, and owing to a long spell of fine weather, he had been so busy stalking that no opportunity had been given him to find time to make his usual visit to the trap after the lapse of a day or two.

Consent was readily given, and on getting to the spot, there they found a splendid golden eagle. He had not been dead very long, for he was quite warm and lissom when taken out; he had been caught by the centre claw only, and it seemed wonderful so powerful a bird had not been able to free himself in his struggles; clearly he had died of exhaustion in his attempts to do so, and not of starvation, for *within reach* of him, and partly eaten, were two grouse and a blue hare, quite freshly killed, with the blood still uncongealed. These could only have been brought to him by *other eagles*— an almost unique instance, I imagine, of sagacity and affection on the part of his comrades, and one which appealed to the hearts of us all. It was a splendid, full-grown bird, and his melancholy end caused my kind host the greatest sorrow; for, by the wish of the noble earl from whom the forest was rented, every effort was made to preserve these beautiful birds, so fast becoming extinct—a wish in which our host most heartily joined, and took every possible care to see carried out.

It is very rare for an eagle at *that time of year*, when there is no difficulty in getting plenty of hares and grouse, to condescend to eat carrion, or anything he has not killed for himself. He was carefully packed up and sent, with a letter of regret and the fullest explanation, to the noble owner of the forest, and I can vouch for it, there are plenty still left; for one could rarely go out in any direction without seeing three or four of these majestic birds, and many a time have I watched their graceful sailings through the spy-glass. It will be a bad day for the poor eagles if once the Rads get their way and abolish the deer-forests; but for the shelter these give, they would already be as extinct as the dodo. On our way to join the ladies, we stopped in the hall to admire again his span of wing and powerful talons; and then a merry round game, followed by a cigar, brought to a close as good a day for all concerned as the most ardent sportsman could desire.

The fate of this silly eagle might well be made to point a moral and adorn a tale, but none of us being great at that sort of thing, it only reminded one of our party of the judge who, summing up a case against an able-bodied young man who lived by stealing poultry, commenced with,—" Prisoner at the bar, Providence has blessed you with the full use of your faculties, and good health and great strength, *instead of which* you go about the world stealing ducks!" and there is no doubt if this poor bird had used the powers he had to get his living by the chase, he would doubtlessly still have been sailing over the three thousand feet of Mount Keen's summit.

CHAPTER X.

A FEW HINTS TO FORESTERS; ANECDOTES OF THEIR GENTLEMEN—CONCLUSION.

WHEREVER it has been my lot to go stalking, I have always found the Scotch forester one of nature's gentlemen. The genuine Highlander has a rooted belief in ghosts and "double goers:" in caverns and pools in which the devil dwells, and though bold as a lion by daylight, nothing would induce him to pass such places after dark. Well do I remember an old forester telling me with bated breath, how one day at a deer drive, he and a friend, early in the morning, but long after sunrise, *both* saw the forester of an adjoining ground approaching them; each knew him well, and thinking he had come to lend a hand at the sport, each hailed him with a shout of welcome: their friend cont'nued to advance until quite close on them, when he suddenly vanished! Strange to say, this story did not wind up with the fact that the man whose apparition had been seen, had died at the very moment of his appearance to his friends. "He was just fretting to be wi' us," was my old friend's explanation; one which appeared natural and satisfactory to him, and in the usual order of events, and who can say for certain that he is so utterly wrong?

Few Highlanders will stay quite alone for many nights in a retired and outlying shooting-lodge: ghosts will appear, and if *they* do not, doors will open and shut of their own accord; bells will ring without hands to pull the bell-rope. I can quite fancy, after a week all alone and not a soul to speak to, and not a neighbour within ten miles, the imagination might easily play tricks with the senses; draughts and winds will open and shut the doors; rats on the wires will set the bells ringing. The caretaker strikes work, and really I think he is right.

In spite of the retired and solitary life many of the Highland foresters lead, he is usually well-informed, and taking an interest in the topics of the day, he is a conversable and pleasant companion, and whether you be duke or commoner, a Mr. Longpurse or a Mr. Shortpurse, he will spare himself no pains or trouble, and take every precaution to give sport and get shots. Willing to explain before setting out on a stalk the movements he intends taking. If he sees you are keen to learn, and show a warm interest, he is also willing to impart as much as he can of his craft in a short time.

Keenly observant, generally a good judge of the character of the gentleman he is with, and a great admirer of a "good plucked one," he is a favourite with all. He will occasionally make remarks which if uttered by Mr. Velveteens in a Norfolk turnip-field would be downright rude, and treated at once as such—not that the Mr. Velveteens of Norfolk or anywhere else are in the habit of forgetting their places, or at all likely to do so. For quite thirty years have I, in almost every county in England, been good friends with English game-keepers, and as a body, a more trustworthy, hard-working, courageous, and civil set of men cannot be found. The whole thing is so different across the Border: for days together you and your stalker are alone, and a good one will, in a variety of small ways and good-natured little attentions to your comfort, make you feel quite friendly towards him; you cannot help seeing that all his thoughts and energies are directed to your sport and comfort. There is something about it all that you instinctively feel is rendered as a pleasure, and into which enters no thought of the tip which, whether ranging from a tenner to a sovereign, according to the depth of your pocket, will be put into his hand when with sorrow you turn from the lodge to drive to the distant station, there to meet the train which will once more take you to your usual and perhaps sedentary avocations.

I have no doubt the English gamekeeper would do as much, and do it as willingly, but he does not get the chance. The gentlemen on this side of the Border who are crack shots, and know all about game preserving, and who would be able, if the keeper was ill, to take the management and beating of their preserves into their own hands, are to be counted by hundreds; but across the Border, in the deer-forests, the gentlemen who know their own ground well enough to be their own stalkers can easily be ticked off on one's fingers.

The Highland forester is usually intensely practical and to the point; withal often very quaint, and his manner is so quiet, and his words so plainly but the utterance of his thought; so evidently spoken without the smallest wish to be discourteous, that it would be churlish to take offence where so clearly none was meant. "Surely you mistook the end of him," he will exclaim, as he sees your bullet strike the haunch instead of the heart. On another occasion we were going to the forest on a very misty morning, determined to go as far as safe, and then wait and chance it clearing up. Suddenly the sun began to show like a moon through the vapour. "Hurrah, Donald! here comes the sun: do you know it is ninety-five millions of miles away?" said the gentleman. "And pray, sir, who went there to measure it?" replies our practical friend, and astronomy not being one of the shooter's strong points, the subject was changed. On the occasion of a picnic to celebrate a lady's birthday, the forester was of course invited, and had peaches, cigarettes, and champagne; the next day he told his master that "they velvet aepples were no bad, and that 'jump wine' was right good, but that tobacco in paper was far too tender for his smoking." As these three luxuries were all novel ties to him, his description was thought decidedly much to the point and very quaint.

In the course of a season's stalking in a forest a stalker will have all sorts of gentlemen under his guidance—fat ones and thin ones, some in condition, some out of it, old hands and novices, some highly excitable, some stolidly phlegmatic, and to stalk for all and each to the best advantage will tax his skill to the utmost. Far be it from me to pretend to teach any forester his business: there are only one or two matters having, however, no direct bearing on his art of stalking on which I will say a word. The first is pace: all stalkers are keen and anxious to show sport, and the days, if they ever existed, have long since passed when they received instructions to take a green hand "out for a walk," and "show him the deer." In their anxiety to get to work they are sometimes apt to forget their gentleman, and start off up-hill at the rate of four miles an hour. It is very poor fun to be toiling two hundred yards behind your stalker; in such a case it is best to sit quietly down, beckon him back to you, and tell him frankly his pace is not yours, that you wish to see as much of the sport as possible, and that therefore you will be obliged to him if he will go a bit slower. Such a hint is very rarely necessary, and once given it will be acted on in the future.

Also a word to the stalker when his gentleman makes a handsome miss. Let him not pick up the rifle and stride off in silence at his best pace, with every muscle set rigid in disgust. If an old hand is out he will sit down and laugh, while he lights his pipe; if it is a novice, it will only make him nervous, and so impress upon him that he has covered himself with disgrace, that he becomes more anxious than ever, and is almost sure to miss again at the next chance. It inspires the misser with far more confidence for future opportunities, and consoles him in some degree for the lost one, if the stalker sit down and take a pipe and a nip with him, and talk the shot over, and tell him where the bullet went if he should happen to have seen it strike; make light of the matter, and tell him of others who have missed, and do all that may be done to restore his confidence, and then the next shot will very likely have a happier termination. It is, I think, Sir Emerson Tennent who writes,—" Whenever I miss I feel like a funeral procession, of which I am the corpse, and the forester, gillie, and pony-man the pall-bearers, and each will be glad to be rid of me before they can again enjoy themselves." The writer quotes only from memory, and if not strictly accurate, it is at any rate the pith of a very excellent description of a party returning from stalking after a good miss or two.

Speaking of missing reminds me of a story that made us all laugh. It happened that the musketry instructor of one of Her Majesty's regiments distinguished himself by a series of misses, and the owner of the forest, in talking the matter over with the head forester, told him of the gallant officer's position; after some moments of reflection the forester sadly remarked, "Well, all I can say is, he'll just spile the shooting of his regiment."

If you are successful, and come home having left a couple of good stags on the hill, do not talk about "two fat deer sixteen stone each" unless you are *certain*, for you will look rather small next day if, when they are put into the larder, the weighing machine says they are barely fourteen stone each; also, if you "fancy" yourself at walking, it will be wiser not to state at the dinner-table, that if your stalker carries the rifle, you never yet met the man who could walk you down, for you will be very apt to meet one the next day who will at any rate have a try, even if he does not succeed. The butler and the footman are usually good friends with the stalker and next day you will find yourself in for a tramp which will considerably astonish you, for these sort of remarks are apt to be taken literally, and the first chance will be seized of having a "feel" at you, just to see what you are made of; there will likely enough be more walking than stalking that day.

The forester is as strict an observer of the Sabbath as the rest of his countrymen, and on one occasion, when a royal personage was invited to cross over the hill for a few days' stalking in an adjoining forest, and selected Sunday for his starting day, in order to be fresh for the Monday's work, all went well up to a certain point; the luggage was packed on the ponies, and all was ready for a start, when the rifle in its mackintosh cover was handed last of all to the forester who was to show the way, and he quietly but respectfully declined to carry it. At last he consented to do so if the rifle were "made into a parcel"; so it was taken to pieces, and the stock and the barrels each packed up separately in brown paper and tied with stout string, and this done the procession started.

One more story of the cannie Scot and I have done. A certain Sassenach, having rented a forest for many years, took such a fancy to it, that on its coming into the market for sale he at once purchased it. For two years after it became absolutely his own he lavished large sums in building a splendid house and making improvements. A miniature Balmoral arose, and then,

I

alas! when all was complete, Mrs. Sassenach took a violent dislike to the place, and would not go there; like a wise man, Mr. Sassenach went alone and took his friends, and the first day he stalked, and during the luncheon "sit" chatted away to his forester, who was an old friend, and had been with him for many years, and at last in a rash moment the master confided his troubles somewhat in this way—"Well, Donald, before I bought this place we came up here eight seasons in succession, and the poor little lodge was good enough, and we were jolly enough in it; but now that the place is mine, and I've spent thousands on building a splendid house, conservatories, stables, and roads, Mrs. Sassenach says she will not stay here—she says it isn't healthy: what do you say?" Donald pauses, takes his pipe from his lips, and like a thunderbolt comes his reply—"She's joost a dommed auld beest!"

Tableaux—Donald dismissed on the spot, and master, swearing hard, goes straight home. In the library five hours later, Donald is very repentant, and humbly asking pardon; master, very stern and frigid, slowly yields, and Donald is to stay; as the door closes behind the downcast but plain-spoken forester, master falls back in his arm-chair shaking from head to foot with laughter.

In these pages the writer has said little on the subject of hind-stalking, as his experience of it has been very limited; neither has he made any mention of deer-driving, as he has never even seen it on a large scale; his nearest approach to it has been in a few chats at Brighton with the much-abused Mr. Winans. That gentleman on one occasion frankly told him that he

CONCLUSION.

was not physically strong enough to undergo the fatigue and hardships of stalking; that his hobby was shooting driven deer, and in order to indulge in this *five or six days a week for six weeks in succession* it was clearly necessary to have an extent of ground so vast, that virtually the deer could not be driven off it. Looking at the matter in this light, the writer sees no reason why Mr. Winans should not be left in peace to enjoy himself in his own way, and he certainly pays very liberally for all the ground he rents.

And now, reader, to wish you good sport, coupling it with the hope that this little essay on a somewhat difficult subject to handle may prove both useful and interesting—interesting enough to while away a sleepless night in the Limited Mail, and useful enough to help you in securing a "royal" or two to grace your dining-room, and give you something to remember with pleasure, when your eyes in after years turn affectionately to the stuffed heads; when perhaps *anno domini* may have you in his clutches; when the hill may no longer be climbed, and the spy-glass and rifle have ceased to see active service, and are kept but to be looked at.

THE END.

RICHARD CLAY & SONS,
BREAD STREET HILL, LONDON,
Bungay, Suffolk.

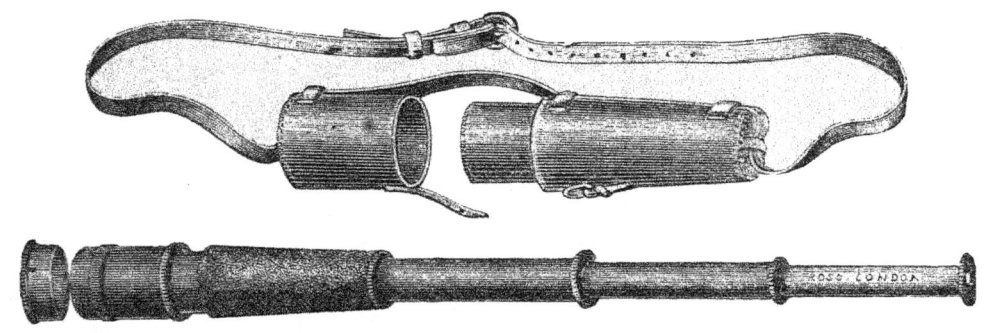

ALUMINIUM TELESCOPES, One-third the Ordinary Weight. Highest Quality & Finish

	DESCRIPTION.	Magnifying Power.	Aperture in Inches.	Area of Light.	No of Draws.	Length Open.	Length Closed.	Brass.
		Times.						£ s.
	Watcher's Telescope, with loops and sling	15	1¼	1·227	2	23¼	10¼	2 15
a	Watcher's Telescope, in sling case	15	1¼	1·227	2	23¼	10¼	3 10
	Reconnoitring Telescope, in sling case	20	1⅜	1·484	3	21	8	4 0
a	Reconnoitring (or Lovat) Telescope, in sling case	20	1⅜	1·484	4	21	6½	4
	Deer-Stalking Telescope, in sling case	20	1½	1·767	3	30½	10¼	5
	Stalking Pancratic Telescope, in sling case	20, 25 & 30	1½	1·767	3	30½	10¼	6 0
c	Deer-Stalking Telescope, in sling case	20	1¾	2·405	3	30	10½	6 15
	Stalking Pancratic Telescope, in sling case	20, 25 & 30	1¾	2·405	3	30	10¾	7 7
	Deer-Stalking Telescope, in sling case	20	2⅛	3·546	3	30½	10½	9

ROSS' POCKET ANEROIDS
AND
HIGH-POWER Binocular Glasses.

Two-Draw (Extra Power) Glass, Bronzed and Covered, £7 0s. £8 0s. £9 10

Two-Draw Aluminium Glass, Extremely Light,   14 0   15 10   17

FULL PARTICULARS ON APPLICATION.

ROSS & CO., Opticians,
112, NEW BOND STREET, LONDON, W.   ESTABLISHED 1830.

PURVEYORS BY SPECIAL WARRANTS TO
H.M. THE QUEEN,
AND
H.R.H. THE PRINCE OF WALES.

BY SPECIAL APPOINTMENT.

BY SPECIAL APPOINTMENT.

SPRATT'S PATENT

MEAT "FIBRINE" VEGETABLE

DOG CAKES

(WITH BEETROOT).   USED IN THE ROYAL KENNELS.

Purveyors to the Kennel Club, Birmingham Nationale, Société St. Hubert, Cercle de la Chasse, Dogs' Home, Battersea, and to all the principal English and Foreign Canine Societies.

SPECIAL NOTICE TO BUYERS.

We regret to find, by the numerous complaints we receive from private gentlemen, that it is more than ever necessary to Caution our Customers to see that, when they order our goods, a cheap and spurious imitation is not supplied them by unprincipled dealers, who thereby make a larger profit.

Please see that every Cake is stamped with the words
"SPRATT'S PATENT" and a **"X."**

Pamphlet on Canine Diseases, and full list of Dog Medicines, post free.

POULTRY MEAL

The most Nutritious and Digestible Food for Chicks and Laying Hens (being thoroughly cooked).

"THE COMMON SENSE OF POULTRY KEEPING," 4d.

GRANULATED PRAIRIE MEAT "CRISSEL."

Takes the place of Insect Life.

Write for our Illustrated Catalogue of Dog, Poultry, Pigeon, and Game Houses, Baskets, Troughs, and Appliances of all kinds, post free.

ADVERTISEMENTS.

SPORT.
By W. BROMLEY DAVENPORT,
Late M.P. for North Warwickshire.

| FOX-HUNTING. | COVERT-SHOOTING. |
| SALMON-FISHING. | DEER-STALKING. |

With numerous Illustrations by Lieut.-General HENRY HOPE CREALOCKE, C.B.
Crown 8vo. 6s.

From THE TIMES.

"We have read the late Mr. Bromley-Davenport's book on 'Sport' with mingled pleasure and regret. We are sorry to think we shall have nothing more from a man who might certainly have made himself a reputation as a writer. A better 'all-round' sportsman never lived, and a brighter volume has seldom been written on sporting subjects. Everywhere we recognise genuine literary talent—a light touch; vividly picturesque descriptions; the gift of describing every day incidents dramatically, with a humorous insight into the natures both of men and beasts. There is a racy freshness in every page, and the practical knowledge brought to the work is unimpeachable. . . . For himself, he was a country gentleman of the best type, who had always lived on kindly terms with the tenantry among whom his ancestors had been settled for some 900 years. Yet Mr. Davenport's literary work, excellent as it is, is run hard by General Crealocke's illustrations. Each of the sketches, while strikingly realistic, is a study of the poetry, the pathos, or the humour of wild animal life. Thus nothing can be more inspiring than the noble group of Highland stags on the frontispiece, voluptuously sniffing the fresh breeze on their native hills, with far-gazing eyes and distended nostrils. . . . General Crealocke's hounds, hares, pheasants, &c., are all equally good; and perhaps the most spirited and original of all are his salmon, seen through the transparent medium of their native element. . . . Paper, print, and illustrations are all that can be desired."

THE RACEHORSE IN TRAINING,
With some Hints on Racing and Racing Reform. To which is added a chapter on "Shoeing."
By WILLIAM DAY.

Fifth Edition. Demy 8vo. 9s.

From THE PALL MALL GAZETTE.

"The chronicles of post and paddock contain scarcely any name either better or longer known than that of Day. What a Day, whether of Danebury, or of Stockbridge, or of Woodyates, has to tell us about the racehorse and pertinent matters is almost as worthy of attention as what a Gamaliel might have to say upon a very different subject. For the Days have been noted jockeys, trainers, and owners from the time of the first 'honest John' to that of 'our William.' And Mr. William Day, who has now added a deed of authorship to his feats of horsemanship, trainership, and ownership, speaks with extraordinary authority upon a certain question of training. He omits sensational anecdotes, though he could no doubt have astonished his readers had be chosen to draw upon his memory for strange stories; and he adopts, on the contrary, a quiet, business-like, simple style, exhibiting here and there an ingenuous disposition quite different from the Machiavellian character which general opinion attributes to the trainer of racehorses."

THE PYTCHLEY BOOK OF REFINED COOKERY AND BILLS OF FARE.
By MAJOR L*****.

Large Crown 8vo. 8s.

From THE SPORTSMAN.

"This is a volume which will be found particularly useful during the approaching hunting season, and to those who are in the habit of giving hunt breakfasts or similar parties it will be invaluable. The author deals with the subject of cookery in a lucid and exhaustive manner, a special feature in the publication being a collection of 'bills of fare,' which comprises twelve for each month of the year. 'Wines and their service' are also dealt with."

LOG-BOOK OF A FISHERMAN AND ZOOLOGIST.
By FRANK BUCKLAND.

With numerous Illustrations. Fifth Thousand. Crown 8vo. 5s.

From THE GRAPHIC.

"We welcome once more the freshest and most genial of the many writers who aim at

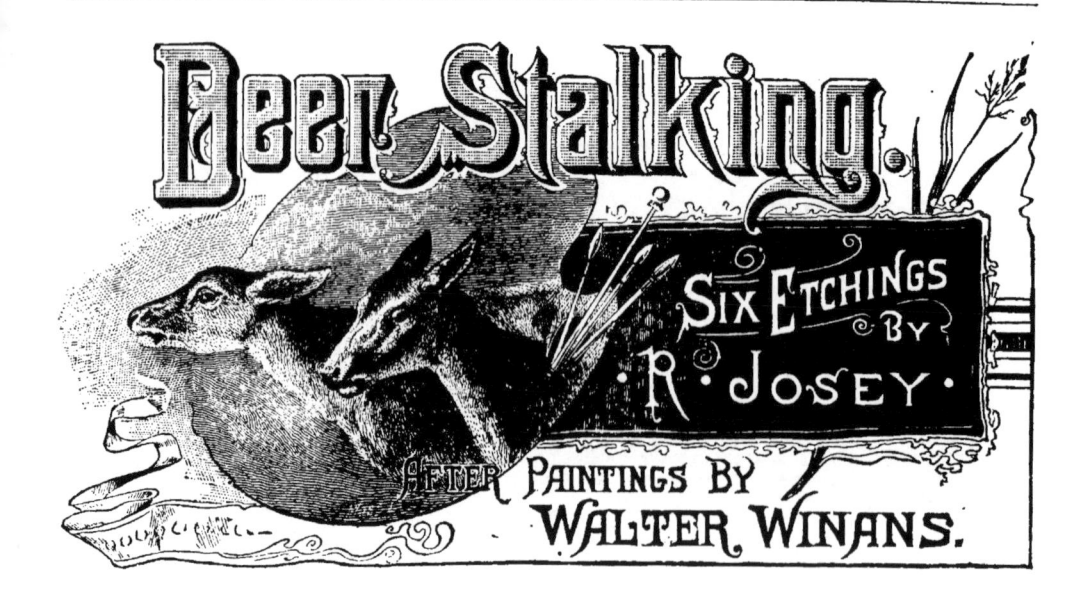

Deer Stalking.
Six Etchings by R. Josey
After Paintings by Walter Winans.

OPINIONS OF THE PRESS.

"We have received these etchings, which are entitled:—(1) 'They're away'; (2) 'A Quiet Shot'; (3) 'A Running Shot'; (4) 'He's very Sick'; (5) 'Greallach'; and (6) 'Returning.' We have never seen more truly inspiriting shooting pictures. One breathes the mountain air when looking at those etchings, and Mr. Winans must be congratulated for the striking lifelike scenes he has depicted. 'They're Away' is simply marvellously good—a remark which fully applies to 'A Running Shot,' possibly the best illustration of Deer we have ever seen. If they meet with the success they deserve, very few sportsmen's homes will be without them, for never has such an artistic and sportsmanlike series been published before."—*Shooting Times*.

".... Mr. Winans is evidently a true sportsman, practically conversant with the subjects he seeks to represent. His treatment of them differs in many respects from that usually adopted by painters of inferior experience. For example, he has not put in the conventional hounds, as he has found that they do more harm than good, frightening all the deer off a beat when let loose after a wounded stag. Mr. Winans makes his 'gun' stalk the deer himself, instead of letting the forester or gillie do all the work, except shooting, as is the practice of too many sportsmen now-a-days. He has also throughout all the pictures aimed at drawing the real action of animals whether walking, trotting, galloping, or leaping. The scenery is picturesquely diversified...."—*Morning Post*.

"Owing to the inaccessibility of their haunts, it has been practically impossible for painters to reproduce on canvas these animals with a true fidelity to nature, and some of even our greatest artists have failed to correctly portray the 'monarch of the forest' as he appears on his native heath. The exceptional facilities which Mr. Winans possesses for accurately portraying 'still hunting' has been turned to the happiest account by the artist..... The drawing is executed in a spirited manner thoroughly true to nature.... 'Greallach' is a lovely bit of Scotch scenery. The whole set of six etchings, forming together a unique illustration of Scotch Deer-stalking, which for correctness of outline, perspective, and fidelity to nature, we have never seen surpassed."—*The American Traveller*.

"They are most excellent representations of a series of charming pictures, and cannot fail to delight the eyes of all lovers of sport. Next to possessing the original paintings, a set of these etchings of Mr. R. Josey ought to receive a place in the house of every sportsman, while as specimens of the etcher's art, they cannot fail to please all who have a taste for good prints."—*The Observer*.

ON VIEW at Messrs. FORES, 41, PICCADILLY, W.

Printed in Great Britain
by Amazon